W9-ASG-073

Unchained Reactions

Chernobyl, *Glasnost,*
and Nuclear Deterrence

Unchained Reactions

Chernobyl, *Glasnost,* and Nuclear Deterrence

Arthur T. Hopkins

1993

National Defense University
Washington, DC

National Defense University Press Publications

To increase general knowledge and inform discussion, NDU Press publishes books on subjects relating to US national security.

Each year, in this effort, the National Defense University, through the Institute for National Strategic Studies, hosts about two dozen Senior Fellows who engage in original research on national security issues. NDU Press publishes the best of this research.

In addition, the Press publishes other especially timely or distinguished writing on national security, as well as new editions of out-of-print defense classics, and books based on University-sponsored conferences concerning national security affairs.

Index prepared by EEI, Inc., of Alexandria, VA.

NDU Press publications are sold by the US Government Printing Office. For ordering information, call (202) 783-3238 or write to the Superintendent of Documents, US Government Printing Office, Washington, DC 20402.

Library of Congress Cataloging in Publication Data

Hopkins, Arthur T., 1949–

Unchained reactions: Chernobyl, *glasnost,* and nuclear deterrence

Arthur T. Hopkins.

p. cm.

Includes bibliographical references and index.

1. Soviet Union—Military policy—Public opinion. 2. Nuclear weapons—Soviet Union—Public opinion. 3. Deterrence (Strategy)—Public opinion. 4. Chernobyl Nuclear Accident, Chernobyl, Ukraine, 1986—Public opinion. 5. *Glasnost.* 6. Public opinion—Soviet Union. I. Title.

UA770.H67 1992 92–10537

355′.0335′47—dc20 CIP

First printing, July 1993. ISBN 0-16-035970-8

In memory of my mother,
Loretta A. Noel Hopkins
1917–1990

Contents

Figures

Foreword

When part of the Chernobyl nuclear power plant exploded in 1986, former President Gorbachev was promoting the wholesale restructuring *(perestroika)* of Soviet society, in part by fostering new thinking and more openness *(glasnost).* As this study shows, the events at Chernobyl could not have occurred at a worse time for Soviet hardliners opposing Gorbachev's reform. The Communist Party's inability to control the public's perception of the aftermath of the Chernobyl disaster reveals how *glasnost* contributed to the eventual independence of the former Soviet republics.

This book recounts a string of significant events that hurried the effects of *glasnost* along: the accident itself, the attempted coverup, the inept efforts to clean up the site, and the growing realization by Soviet citizens of what had really happened. The author shows how the bureaucracy's inadequate response to the disaster has exacerbated public distrust of government and brought home another reality—the horrible effects of nuclear disaster.

The Chernobyl disaster continues to affect the way citizens of the defunct Soviet empire think about nuclear power and nuclear war. Thanks to Gorbachev's reforms the voice of the people is now reflected in the policies of Russia and the other new republics. It is apparent from such recent events as US-Russian agreements on drastic nuclear cuts, and the Ukraine's alleged renunciation of nuclear power status, that the effects of democratization are making themselves felt. Barring a resurgence of reactionary forces in Russia and the Ukraine—which is not impossible—the tragedy of Chernobyl may have contributed to that most worthy of goals—deterrence of nuclear war.

PAUL G. CERJAN
Lieutenant General, US Army
President, National Defense University

Preface

The guard at Mitinskoye Cemetery, one of Moscow's newest, was closing the main gate just as we pulled up. We would have arrived sooner if the taxi driver hadn't taken a few wrong turns along the way. The Moscow native stopped twice to ask for directions to the cemetery, first at a bus stop where a group of commuters pointed in four different directions, then at a busy Gorky Street intersection where a Red Army soldier explained how to reach Mitinskoye. The cabbie thanked the soldier, made a U-turn across four lanes, and made up for lost time by weaving his Russian Volga subcompact through the evening rush hour traffic like a Keystone Kop. I braced myself by grabbing the dashboard. Seat belts probably hadn't been an option to the car's original owner; neither, apparently, were windshield wipers, headlights, or shock absorbers.

We arrived just at sunset—with barely enough light to take photographs of the Chernobyl Heroes' Monument that I'd read about in Soviet newspaper articles. Running from the car to the cemetery gate, we encountered the guard. After a few minutes of animated debate between the taxi driver and the guard (during which I heard the word "Americanski" several times), the guard not only let us in, but also directed us to the area where 26 of Chernobyl's victims were buried. I wanted to see and photograph the Soviet monument to the bravery and selflessness of firefighters and reactor operators who had been among the first to die from the effects of the Chernobyl accident. I also expected to see grave sites with decorations left over from the previous day's May Day ceremonies. In the Russian Orthodox tradition, survivors often honor the dead by transforming grave sites into flower gardens, some with photographs of the deceased mounted on headstones.

There was no monument. Its design had been completed in 1987 (figure 1), but it hadn't been built out of fear that the memorial might be construed as honoring the "bungling and negligence" of the reactor operators, those "virtual criminals" that many Soviets felt were responsible for the disaster. There weren't many decorated graves, either. In fact, less than a year earlier, the photographs of all but one of the reactor operators had been removed in symbolic protest over their burial among Chernobyl's "true heroes," the firefighters. (That reactor operator was one of the youngest victims, apparently excused from blame by virtue of his age and inexperience—figure 2.) Such polarization of opinion about a simple monument and a gravestone decoration signifies how deeply the Chernobyl accident has affected Soviet people's attitudes. The accident was much more invasive than many Westerners are aware. It directly affected hundreds of thousands of lives, and millions of people's opinions.

In the wake of their government's failed (but mercifully short-lived) coverup attempt, many Soviets remain quite skeptical of their leadership, scientists, and nuclear technology. Many perceive the accident as a "top down" disaster. Not surprisingly, many of the accident's lessons are being drawn by the people from the "bottom up." They have learned much from their misfortune; they want to strengthen their capacity to prevent and, if necessary, recover from future disasters, including nuclear war.

This book focuses on a largely overlooked aspect of Chernobyl's influence on people's attitudes. It examines how the accident affected deterrence and the way people think about nuclear war. Deterrence is, after all, a frame of mind, an attitude. As much as possible, I relied on Soviet writings to understand and convey their attitudes. Thanks to the prevailing policy of openness

FIGURE 1. *Design of Chernobyl Heroes' Monument*

FIGURE 2. *Chernobyl operator's grave site at Mitinskoye Cemetery*

(*glasnost*), I found no shortage of Soviet opinions about Chernobyl and its effects on citizens' lives and attitudes about nuclear deterrence. Even the story about the monument links the Chernobyl accident with deterrence. The unbuilt monument's design, a mushroom cloud behind the figure of a person with outstretched arms, dramatically relates Chernobyl to the effects of nuclear war.

The accident undoubtedly made nuclear war less thinkable, strengthening deterrence by increasing the Soviets' fears of nuclear weapon effects. Interestingly, though, it may also have weakened deterrence by increasing the Soviets' confidence in their ability to recover from war's aftermath. There is evidence of both attitudes in their literature.

Which attitude will prevail in public policy? If *perestroika* leads to democratization and pluralism in policymaking, then the attitudes of those millions of people affected by Chernobyl could ultimately influence future policy. If news reports and other literature are a barometer, Chernobyl will strengthen deterrence.

Acknowledgments

I thank Dr. Fred Kiley, the Director of the National Defense University Press, and Dr. Joe Goldberg, Professor of Research, for their considerate and generous assistance from the very start of this project. Fred's sage advice really did make the research easy and the writing enjoyable. Joe supported my efforts daily with material and moral support. His contributions, encouragement, and frequent intellectual challenges added significantly to the academic rigor of my research. I am especially grateful to Mr. Tom Gill, editor and writer with the National Defense University Press, for his expert commentary and the editorial support he provided to prepare this book for publication.

While writing this book, I was very fortunate to have travelled to the Soviet Union with a small group of National Defense University students and faculty. I am indebted to Dr. Milt Kovner, our group leader and Professor of Political Science at the Industrial College of the Armed Forces (ICAF), for helping me to deviate from the group's itinerary in order to visit Mitinskoye Cemetery near Moscow. Milt also translated my Chernobyl-related questions to various Soviet military officers and Friendship Society members.

I am truly grateful for the willing and authoritative contributions from people at ICAF and other organizations. Dr. Ed Hullander, Professor of Economics at ICAF, helped me express the accident's recovery costs in terms of a Soviet Gross National Product. Dr. John Bokel, ICAF Professor and Federal Emergency Management Agency Chair, provided comparisons of US and Soviet Civil Defense programs. Dr. David Auton, at the Defense Nuclear

Agency, helped me start the research by identifying references and contacts for interviews. Dr. Leon Goure of Science Applications International Corporation kindly contributed to my understanding of the accident's scope by sharing key references and videotapes of foreign documentaries about Chernobyl. My friend and neighbor, Joe Yardumian, greatly assisted the research by citing references and facilitating contacts with his fellow Nuclear Regulatory Commission experts and others who have been involved in Chernobyl studies and joint US–USSR programs.

My family saw how demanding this effort has been. Thanks to my children, Sarah and Patrick, for understanding. Above all, I thank my wife, Jeannie. I could not have written this book without her complete support and involvement. She reviewed my work with the skill and patience of a teacher. Her thoughtful, constructive critiques added a lot to the book's clarity.

Unchained Reactions

Chernobyl, *Glasnost,*
and Nuclear Deterrence

Deterrence Before Chernobyl

IN LATE APRIL 1986, one of four nuclear reactors in a remote Ukrainian village exploded, then burned for 10 days. It was not a nuclear explosion, but the smoke plume from the burning reactor core did contain radioactive particles from the fuel rods. The radioactive cloud contaminated large areas of the Ukraine and Belorussia, covering much of Europe before winds scattered its fallout throughout the entire northern hemisphere. Thousands of people were hurt; millions were affected—none more than the Soviets. Hundreds of thousands of Soviet citizens were forced from their homes. In a real way, the accident altered the courses of their lives: their professions, environments, and attitudes.

The Soviets' firsthand experiences with widespread fear, radiation sickness, decontamination, and evacuations simply had to influence the way they think. Not surprisingly, many have lost faith in their nuclear industries; they openly question the acceptability of nuclear power's demonstrated risks despite its much needed benefits. The accident fueled the nuclear power debate outside the Soviet Union, as well. However, Chernobyl affected more than just the way people think about nuclear power.

The reactor accident also affected people's attitudes about nuclear war. Chernobyl's principal environmental insult was its radioactive contamination, and contamination is a feared effect of nuclear war. Like the Japanese survivors of Hiroshima and Nagasaki, the people who survived Chernobyl think about war differently now.[1] By affecting Soviet attitudes about nuclear war, Chernobyl affected nuclear deterrence, the threat of war to ensure peace.

Deterrence Theories

Strategic analysts in both the United States and the Soviet Union (thanks in part to the new *glasnost*) have generated a formidable body of scholarly literature analyzing deterrence theory as well as its attendant military strategies and force structures. The very concept of deterrence has been controversial, to say the least. Strategic analyst Michael Nacht explains the appeal and persistence of deterrence: "as unnerving and as dangerous as nuclear deterrence has been, there are at present no plausible and preferrable alternatives to it."[2]

Deterrence is as inelegant as it is effective: it prevents nuclear war by threatening it. Since the end of World War II, the United States has threatened to use nuclear weapons if vital interests were jeopardized. Soviet Communist leaders had to believe that unacceptable retaliatory damage would be a certain consequence of any military aggression. Deterrence has been a basic element of US defense strategy supporting the national strategy of containment.[3]

Fear of self-destruction has worked. It has successfully prevented the world's nuclear powers from militarily engaging each other directly, and it has defused their indirect military engagements because of the potential for escalation. For more than 40 years, deterrence has controlled not only US defense strategy but also the evolution of military forces.

The success of deterrence depends very much on forces: the military *capability* to make good on the threat of nuclear war. Both the United States and the Soviet Union have aggressively modernized their nuclear forces since the end of World War II. Each side perceives the other as capable of nuclear retaliation—and they are about evenly matched. The Soviets are convinced that they need nuclear parity with the United States in order to deter "those crazy Americans" who believe that 150 million casualties would constitute a favorable outcome of nuclear war.[4]

Rough military parity implies a condition of stability in the sense that neither side has the upper hand, or has anything to win by starting a nuclear war. However, this US view of deterrence and stability requires "informed, rational, and coherent decisionmaking" by an enemy to prevent war.[5] If, as history suggests, the United States really can't count on the enemy to think in a way that supports the US concept of deterrence, is deterrence a reliable strategy? Without knowing *intentions,* deterrence could fail, even if force parity exists. Uncertainty about intentions, purely psychological aspects of deterrence, have focused much of the US public debate on the *credibility* of deterrence.

The success of deterrence depends very much on its credibility. Soviet decisionmakers have to believe that the United States could and would use nuclear weapons if necessary. The quest for credibility has driven the evolution of US military strategy. Massive retaliation was fine when no one else had nuclear weapons. Once others had them, however, self-destruction became an almost certain consequence of their use. How credible is a strategy that virtually guarantees national suicide?

Attempting to diminish that suicidal aspect of nuclear deterrence and to strengthen its credibility, US strategists devised policies that called for restraint. In the event of war, they wanted to have nuclear options other than inaction or Armageddon. The policy of flexible response is supposed to fill that need. It gives US national command authorities a spectrum of military response options, including nuclear retaliation at any level of conflict. Potential enemies know those options exist, so fear of reprisal and unilateral escalation deters all levels of agression.

The need for credibility introduces a paradox, though. A credible nuclear strategy for deterrence could make a nuclear war *more* likely.[6] A truly believable nuclear deterrent strategy increases the chances that nuclear weapons will actually be used, because credibility requires expansion of the opportunities for using them, especially in flexible response options. Credibility also invites preemption because it leaves the enemy with no hope for survival unless they go first.[7] In theory anyway, strengthening deterrence may actually weaken it. However, there's little evidence that the Soviets believe the US theory of deterrence at all, much less the paradox of credibility.

In his book about Soviet strategic thought, Roman Kolkowitz asserts, "Soviet analysts find Western strategic sophistries objectionable and unacceptable on several grounds."[8] The US focus on mutual suicide has precluded serious US considerations of victory. Suicide hasn't dominated Soviet thinking. According to strategic analyst Colin S. Gray, "The dominant Soviet idea of victory in an undesired World War III encompasses expectations of human and economic losses that the United States deems incompatible with a meaningful concept of victory."[9] The Soviets never have accepted mutual vulnerability as responsible national policy. They believe that nuclear war cannot possibly be limited; escalation cannot be controlled. However, their literature indicates that Soviet academics (evidently, former Communists) can't decide "whether thermonuclear war would mean the end of civilization or just the end of capitalism."[10] They interpret the West's flexible response as a NATO scheme for dominance in European battles.

Furthermore, in Communist eyes, the essence of US deterrence theory is support for the status quo. To a Marxist-Leninist society that was ideologically steeped in the dialectic of change, that is anathema. They believe that they can best deter nuclear war by preparing to fight and win it. Preparation is their quest for credibility.

According to Harvard history professor Richard Pipes, the Soviet military unequivocally rejects US notions that nuclear weapons could inflict unacceptable damage. Having suffered nearly 30 million casualties and the destruction of over 70,000 villages in their Great Patriotic War (World War II), only to recover and emerge as a world power, the Soviets are not likely to be "intimidated by the prospect of destruction."[11] The Soviets have been preparing to fight the next war ever since the end of the last war.

Preparation means denying their enemies any chance of winning. It means doing whatever it takes to fight and win. In a nuclear war, winning includes mere survival. Survival demands enough military force for preemption, and the ability to recover after the war. Fighting to win and planning to recover are the lessons of bitter experience.

The Soviets' Great Patriotic War experience was far more influential than a set of theories or textbook lessons. Combat experience has driven the development of their society's "cult of militarism."[12] Starting with paramilitary youth clubs, they instill paranoia and xenophobia to foster patriotism. From childhood, citizens learn the value of strong, brave military forces: forces that have successfully defended the motherland in the past, and, in all liklihood, will have to again. They immortalize and revere war heroes the way that Christians do saints.

Brave soldiers are not sufficient, however, to deter or fight a nuclear battle. Experience has also taught them how important it is to plan for *recovery* after a war. Recovery from nuclear war calls for far-reaching plans to protect leaders, citizens, and industries from the immediate and long-term effects of nuclear weapons. The Soviet military's strong emphasis on Civil Defense is thoroughly consistent with their view that it is "a critical 'strategic factor' which, in a large measure, can determine the course and outcome of a nuclear war."[13] Because recovery is essential to fighting and winning, it is an essential aspect of the Soviet concept of deterrence.

Recovery from Chernobyl

The Soviets actually approached the Chernobyl accident like a military challenge, using thousands of military troops to help control the burning reactor and to recover from the effects of its widespread radioactive contamination. Soviet writers and politicians frequently compared the accident's radioactive contamination to the hypothetical effects of a nuclear war. The accident became a benchmark, a basis for mental extrapolation to the effects of war. Describing the military's assistance in the recovery, a *Pravda* reporter at Chernobyl referred to the accident scene metaphorically as a battlefield:

> The fact that the Armed Forces have been assigned a substantial portion of the work of eliminating the consequences of the accident at the nuclear power station again underscores the size of the disaster that has hit all of us . . . servicemen from special chemical-defense units and civil-defense groups have worked here. . . . Battlefield operations are continuing.[14]

The Soviets fought the accident like a battle; the burning reactor and its radioactive plume were the enemies. They used military troops in the battle.

Thousands, maybe millions, of citizens were also affected. Most importantly, they considered Chernobyl's widespread contamination to be a relatively small-scale version of one effect of a nuclear war, one that their technology failed to deter.

Chernobyl may actually have weakened deterrence if their experience with recovery gave the Soviets confidence in their ability to recover from a nuclear war. As psychologist Steven Kull's interviews with Soviet military authorities revealed, victory-oriented thinking was still prevalent among their most influential citizens in 1968.[15] Like their Great Patriotic War experience, their Chernobyl "combat" experience has shaped the way the Soviets think about nuclear war and recovery from it. It affected deterrence.

Deterrence relies on fear: the fear of retaliation inhibits the use of nuclear weapons. Chernobyl also convinced people that the magnitude of effects from nuclear retaliation would be much more fearful, more widespread and longer lived than was conceivable from theories. In that sense, it strengthened deterrence. During the accident's early stages, 31 people were killed; 200 more died within 4 years; and tens of thousands of people will probably die from Chernobyl's lingering radioactive contamination.[16] The body count doesn't begin to describe the disruptive effects of evacuating and resettling hundreds of thousands of Soviet citizens, and treating people suffering from nonlethal radiation sickness, both real and imagined.

To appreciate the scope of Chernobyl's influence on deterrence, though, it is necessary to understand the accident itself and the events that surrounded it. What exactly happened? Who got hurt? How did the Soviet government and opinion leaders respond at a time when they were trying to restructure their society with the "new thinking" of *perestroika*? How did the accident influence the way people think about nuclear war, about deterrence?

Answers and Analyses

This book analyzes Chernobyl's influence on Soviet attitudes about nuclear war and its deterrence. It explores their literature to reveal those attitudes. Since Chernobyl, Soviet literature has been a fertile, accessible source of information and opinion. After a brief attempt at cover-up, *glasnost*—or openness—prevailed, and Soviet reporters, scientists, and military writers revealed many facts, investigated inequities, and published a surprisingly diverse assortment of opinions about Chernobyl and its effects. Soviet sources are used liberally in this book to convey *the Soviets'* thoughts and opinions. After all, their thinking underlies the US policy of deterrence.

Soviet literature strongly suggests that Soviet strategic thought is much less sophisticated and convoluted than its US counterpart. Whether the Soviets think they can "fight and win" a nuclear war is a highly debatable question. So is whether the US really could impose restraint on the process of conflict escalation through its policy of "flexible response." Soviet literature suggests that US plans for escalation control were interpreted as plans to dominate Europe militarily in a crisis. Nevertheless, Chernobyl taught the Soviets some hard lessons about the ultimate consequences of unbridled escalation.

Chapter 1, "The Ukrainian Syndrome," describes how hard those lessons were. The accident was far more catastrophic and far reaching than Americans generally perceive. Furthermore, it truly stunned the Soviet people. Two months before the accident, *Soviet Life* magazine boldly asserted that a nuclear power plant accident was impossible in the Soviet Union. The Chernobyl power plant epitomized modern, safe technology in an advanced Communist society. Chapter 1 explains how the impossible happened, what happened, and how much cleanup will cost.

Cleaning it up, or "eliminating the consequences" as the Soviets put it, has required the assistance and cooperation of many nations, several of whom conditioned their cooperation on the Soviets' complete, open, and truthful reporting of all aspects of the accident. Not surprisingly, it has been argued that the accident practically induced *glasnost,* but it didn't materialize instantly. Communist society was long accustomed to concealing negative publicity from its own citizens as well as the rest of the world, and the facts of the accident emerged slowly. Chapter 2, "The Strained Evolution of *Glasnost,*" describes this development.

Ultimately, Soviet literature did convey a real sense of the accident's true magnitude and its influence on peoples' lives and attitudes. *Glasnost* started in earnest with the Soviet report to the International Atomic Energy Agency Conference in Vienna 4 months after Chernobyl, and continues to the present. Diaries of Valerii Legasov, the now deceased Soviet nuclear physicist and a commissioner in charge of the cleanup, and Grigoriy Medvedev, a reporter who interviewed terminally ill victims of the accident, gave first-person recollections of events and peoples' reactions. Chapter 3 traces how they and other writers recounted the events of Chernobyl, and how they perceived the incident's influence on people's attitudes. Their stories reveal that the Chernobyl experience has affected people in ways that could both strengthen and weaken deterrence. The accident obviously added to the fear of war, but it also may have improved people's confidence in an already impressive capacity to recover from war. The ability to recover is absolutely essential for them to "fight and win" (in their minds, to deter) a nuclear war.

Chapter 4 explores how Chernobyl may have actually weakened the deterrence of nuclear war. The Soviets fought the accident like a military campaign—they used military troops and nuclear decontamination equipment and techniques. At the very least, they learned how effective their civil defense system would be under conditions much less stressing than a nuclear war. At most, they can apply Chernobyl's lessons about decontamination, evacuation, and medical response to improve their already robust defenses. Soviet writings include evidence that they did exactly that; they improved their civil defense plans, decontamination methods, medicines, and agricultural recovery techniques. Better defenses could lead to more confidence in a crisis and less fear of escalation to nuclear war. If so, Chernobyl weakened deterrence.

On the other hand, as a mere glimpse of nuclear war's aftereffects, the Chernobyl accident demonstrated how difficult recovery really would be. Chapter 5, "Stronger Deterrence," cites ample evidence from Soviet literature that the accident strengthened deterrence by hurting and scaring millions of people. One tangible result of Chernobyl's deterrence-strengthening lessons may have been the Soviets' ratification of a 1977 Geneva Protocol that outlaws nuclear reactor attacks. Along with 101 other nations, they signed the Protocol in 1977. But they waited until after Chernobyl, 12 years after signing the Protocol, to ratify it. The United States has not yet ratified it because of concerns about its enforceability, and objections to other aspects of the Protocol that would legitimize terrorists by defining them as combatants in national liberation struggles. Soviet writers also make it clear that not everyone in the Soviet Union embraced Chernobyl's deterrence-weakening lessons discussed in Chapter 4. Their highly touted civil defense system was so ill prepared and so disorganized that many Soviets argued that they could *never* reasonably expect civil defense to protect society from the aftereffects of a nuclear war.

The last chapter, "After Chernobyl," examines the question of what lessons Soviet citizens *want* to learn. If democratization flourishes in the process of restructuring (*perestroika*), then Chernobyl's ultimate lesson may be what the majority of their citizens *want* it to be. Overall, their stunningly open post-Chernobyl literature clearly indicates that they are now more fearful of the effects of a nuclear war, and less confident of their ability to recover from one. Thus, Chernobyl strengthened nuclear deterrence more than weakened it.

1. "The Ukrainian Syndrome"

THE ACCIDENT at the Chernobyl nuclear power station was not like previous large Soviet disasters; it could not be rapidly and quietly contained as an isolated tragedy and hidden from most Soviet citizens and the rest of the world. It was, rather, a widely felt, messy event that not only affected, but also violently changed, the lives of hundreds of thousands of Soviet citizens. Furthermore, if medical predictions are right, the accident's radioactive fallout will prematurely end the lives of tens of thousands of people in the Northern Hemisphere.

Before the Chernobyl accident happened, Soviet authorities referred indirectly to the popular book and movie, *The China Syndrome,* when they mockingly labeled some Ukrainian residents' fears and resistance to the Chernobyl power station, "The Ukrainian Syndrome." Nowhere has the impact of the accident been more profound than in the Soviet Ukraine.

Chernobyl and the Ukraine

Named after a 12th-century Ukrainian settlement, the town of Chernobyl (Russian for wormwood[1]) sits 16 kilometers to the southeast of the nuclear power station. The station's neighbors were proud to host such a powerful, visible symbol of the Soviet Union's commitment to Ukrainian development and modernization. Memories of military invasions, religious repression, man-made famines, and Stalin's purges linger, burdening Ukrainian nationals with a sense of second-class citizenship. The power station at Chernobyl was supposed to help diminish that feeling.

From Lenin's comment—"If we lose the Ukraine, we lose our head"—to Gorbachev's—"You can only imagine what would happen if there were disorder in the Ukraine. Fifty-one million people live here. The whole fabric of the Soviet Union would be amiss, and *perestroika* would fail"—Soviet leaders have long demonstrated that they recognize the importance of the Ukraine.[2] Only Russia is a larger republic in the Soviet Union. The Chernobyl power station was one of several modern nuclear power plants built in the Ukraine, and it was an important element in the long-term Soviet plan for nuclear energy development in that populous Soviet European republic.

The Ukraine has more nuclear power plants than any other Soviet republic; the plan was (and still is) to build more. It was the first republic in the Soviet Union to build a nuclear power plant (at Odessa, on the Black Sea) for both electrical power and steam heat for vegetable farming, fish and poultry farming, and irrigation. The Ukraine's energy pioneering was the topic of a sadly ironic series of feature articles in *Soviet Life* magazine just two months before the accident at Chernobyl. The stories emphasized how safe nuclear power was in the Soviet Union and gushed with praise for the Chernobyl power station and its bedroom community, Pripyat:

> The odds of a meltdown are one in 10,000 years. . . . The plants have safe and reliable controls that are protected from any breakdown. . . . Professions and trades concerned with servicing nuclear equipment are also growing in popularity in the Ukraine. Young people come to us willingly.[3]

* * *

> Fifteen years ago the town of Pripyat wasn't on a map of the Ukraine. It owes its birth to the Chernobyl nuclear power plant. . . . The town of Pripyat should be as safe and clean as the power plant. . . . Working at the plant is safer than driving a car. . . . Both man and nature are completely safe. . . . Even if the unpredictable should happen, the automatic control and safety systems would shut down the reactor in a matter of seconds. . . . There is more emotion in fear of nuclear power plants than real danger.[4]

* * *

> In the 30 years since the first Soviet nuclear power plant opened [in Obninsk on June 27, 1954] there has not been a single instance when plant personnel or nearby residents have been seriously threatened; not a single disruption in normal operation occurred that would have resulted in the contamination of the air, water, or soil.[5]

It's certainly no wonder the Ukrainians confidently hosted the Chernobyl power station. However, B. I. Oleinik of the Ukraine Republic Writers' Union revealed some nationalist resentment over the way Moscow executed the Ukraine's nuclear energy program:

> The arrogance and disdain that some Union bodies, especially the Ministry of Power and Electrification, show toward the Ukraine's fate border not only on sort of merciless cruelty, but on an insult to national dignity. I recall how some people, in pushing through the construction of the Chernobyl Nuclear Power Station, chuckled at the "Ukrainian syndrome," saying: This is so safe, you could install the reactor under a newlywed's bed.[6]

Explosions, Fires, and Contamination

The Chernobyl reactor's poor design and poorly trained operators collaborated to show how absurd the safety claims really were. At 1:23 in the morning on Saturday, April 26, 1986, explosions literally raised the roof, a 1,000-ton cover plate, over reactor number four in the Chernobyl power station. Explosions occurred while operators were conducting unauthorized experiments, ironically aimed at improving reactor safety. They were trying to show how they could sustain power to the reactor's emergency safety systems in the event of an unexpected loss of power to the generator that normally energized those safety systems.

The Chernobyl reactor is a uniquely Soviet design, called "RBMK" by the nuclear reactor community. Loosely translated, RBMK is an acronym of Russian words that mean "reactor, high power, channel-type or pressure tube." RBMK reactors are not used in the West; they are perceived to have (at least) three undesirable design features. First, the system that is supposed to shut the reactor down is too slow. Second, the reactor is intrinsically unstable when operated at low power levels, like the levels required for the ill-fated experiment. Third, there are no "failsafe" mechanisms to prevent operators from putting the reactor into its unstable condition.[7] These weaknesses, along with operator misjudgments, produced the Chernobyl reactor accident.

The operators turned off critical safety systems and reduced the flow of cooling water as they reduced the reactor's power levels. The low water flow was insufficient to remove excess heat caused by the nuclear reactions. The heat quickly evaporated water, producing steam in the reactor's coolant channels. It is a feature of the Chernobyl reactor's design that the presence of steam in the core causes power to increase, which in turn produces more steam and more power. Reactor power increased unchecked, somewhere between 100 to 500 times normal, disintegrating fuel assemblies and generating very high pressure.[8]

There were two explosions. The first, a steam explosion, blew the 1,000-ton concrete and steel lid off the reactor. The second, a hydrogen explosion caused by chemical reactions within the breached reactor, launched chunks of radioactive fuel, radioactive waste products, and burning graphite over the surrounding area. The burning graphite came from the reactor's core—a stack of graphite blocks, perforated by vertical openings for uranium fuel rods and control rods. When operating, uranium atoms in the fuel rods are split by neutrons liberated by the preceding uranium fission reactions. Those liberated neutrons have to be moderated, or slowed down, before they can split other atoms. The graphite core is the moderating material. Operators use the control rods as neutron absorbers to throttle the chain reaction process by raising or lowering them into or out of the core.[9]

After the explosions, fire became the immediate problem; the other reactors had to be protected. Reactor number four's graphite reactor core was burning out of control, lofting radioactive particles in its plume of combustion byproducts, while the burning graphite fragments launched by the explosion started approximately 30 fires in different areas of the power plant.[10]

Within 5 minutes of the explosions (recall that the accident happened at 1:23 a.m.), local firefighters were alerted and on their way to the power station. When they got there, they saw heavy, billowing smoke illuminated by flames on the station's roof. To extinguish the blaze, firemen had to stand on the 30-meter-high roof. The height was only one of the many difficulties they faced as they tried to control the fire. One eyewitness said,

> the roof's bitumen was melting, so their boots became heavier every minute and got stuck in the molten mass turning to "lead" from the tar sticking to them.[11]

The smoke was not just noxious, it was radioactive. Of the 31 casualties, 28 died from radiation,

2 died of burns, and 1 suffered a heart attack while fighting fires.[12]

The firefighters' efforts were truly heroic and largely successful: the other reactors were spared extensive fire damage. However, the damaged reactor's graphite core continued to burn for days. Almost 24 hours after the explosion, as government commissioners approached Chernobyl on the road from Kiev, they

> were taken aback by the appearance of the sky. At a distance of some 8–10 km [5 or 6 miles] from the station we could see a crimson glow . . . it looked like a metallurgical plant or a major chemical enterprise over which there hung a huge crimson glow covering half the sky.[13]

The commission had been sent to find out what was happening, to develop and implement a plan to control events, and to order evacuations, if necessary. Unaware that the fuel rods had been disintegrated by the explosions, commission members first had to learn whether the reactor was still producing neutrons that could sustain nuclear fission reactions (a "critical" condition). Entering the reactor building in an armored personnel carrier, they measured neutron levels that were insufficient to support an assumption that the reactor was still operating. They deduced that the burning graphite core was the only significant source of heat at that time.

Intense heat and radioactivity levels made it impossible to extinguish the graphite fire from the ground, so forces had to fight it from the air. The burning graphite had to be cooled and suffocated—

traditional means such as water and foam could not be used. In the 10 days it took to suffocate the graphite fire, helicopters dropped more than 5,000 tons of lead, sand, clay, dolomite, and boron carbide onto the damaged reactor. To minimize their radiation exposure, helicopter pilots developed the technique of dropping a 10-ton netful of material onto the reactor without hovering, flying an aerobatic slalom 200 meters above the station at more than 80 miles per hour. The sand for the firefighting effort was dredged from the nearby Pripyat River.

The Pripyat River was the focus of intense concern throughout the Chernobyl disaster. It is a source of drinking water for millions of Ukrainians, and it feeds the Dnepr River, the water supply for millions of residents of Kiev, the republic's capital. Fear of radioactive contamination motivated extraordinary efforts to monitor Pripyat water, to control runoff from nearby contaminated soil, and to prevent rains from occurring over local drainage basins. Soviet scientists seeded clouds far upwind of Chernobyl to reduce the likelihood of rain over the contaminated areas. They built embankments along the sides of the river to control runoff of contaminated water. The Soviets even dug 58 new artesian wells near Kiev for drinking water, and 73 new wells in an area to the south of the power station to intercept potentially contaminated ground water before it reached the Pripyat River.[14] Potentially contaminated water and air were important concerns that led to decisions to evacuate thousands of local residents.

Evacuations

The town of Pripyat, a bedroom community built primarily for power plant workers, was the first to be evacuated. More than 1,100 buses came from Kiev to remove over 45,000 people from Pripyat alone. However, those evacuations didn't start until 36 hours after the explosion, because local Communist Party officials were unable to understand the magnitude of the disaster, and to take decisive action. It was left to the special commissioners from Moscow to take control.

Reactor management officials (Communist Party members, of course) were later punished severely for their involvement and indecisiveness. For example, the power station's former director, V. Bryukhanov, was tried, convicted, and sentenced to the maximum 10 years' "deprivation of freedom" for negligent behavior. His crimes included failure to "implement the plan for protecting personnel and the public from radiation . . . delaying the prompt evacuation of people from the danger zone."[15]

Looking back, though, the delay for which many were punished may have been fortuitous for the residents of Pripyat and neighboring communities. Early Saturday morning, following the explosion, winds were carrying the radioactive smoke plume directly over the main evacuation routes. By Sunday afternoon, winds had changed; Pripyat was downwind of the burning reactor, and the evacuation routes were relatively safe.[16]

The overwhelming majority of evacuees came from within a 30-kilometer (18.6-mile) radius of the Chernobyl power station. More than 135,000 people were moved from the 30-kilometer zone during the first week after the accident. Townspeople were easier to move than farmers, who wouldn't readily abandon their livestock, so 1,500 trucks and livestock haulers scoured the countryside picking up cows and pigs. Drivers had to wear respirators and special protective clothing. Later, the haulers and trucks had to be decontaminated (as did *all* vehicles used in the 30-kilometer zone). This evacuation of the countryside, out to 60 kilometers by some accounts, is referred to by local residents as the "second evacuation."[17]

Today, the 30-kilometer zone has not yet been completely repopulated, and it is not likely that it will be soon. A completely new city, Slauvitch, has been built to house Chernobyl power station workers and their families (the other three reactors are back up and running). Pripyat will not be habitable until decontamination efforts and the natural radioactive decay process reduce the danger to acceptable levels. The entire 30-kilometer zone is now encircled with a barbed wire fence to help control access to the most radioactive areas.[18] The Soviets must continuously monitor and try to decontaminate those areas. Evacuations may still be necessary for some villages outside the 30-kilometer zone if future analyses suggest that there could be serious risks to people, livestock, and crops.

Risks

Risk assessment is difficult, imprecise, and controversial. Soviet officials have made decisions to evacuate citizens only after analyses of fallout data suggest that people might be exposed to radiation levels that would be unsafe in the long run. Soviet authorities estimate that most evacuees received a radiation dose less than 25 Rem.[19] Rem is an acronym for "Roentgen equivalent man," a measure of how much of the energy (in the form of invisible light rays) from radioactive fallout would actually be absorbed by human tissue during the time that the tissue is bathed in the radiation.

With a dose less than 25 Rem, acute radiation sickness, requiring immediate treatment or hospitalization, was not expected. People did complain of symptoms that authorities ascribed to a "radiophobia, whereby people typically linked the most common of maladies with the consequences of the Chernobyl accident".[20] The Soviets have tried to combat this radiophobia and emotional distress among the affected population with psychological and emotional counseling and psychiatric therapy.

While the low radiation doses probably didn't cause immediate pain, 25 Rem and even lower doses *can* increase the probability of cancer later in life. Over the next 70 years, a few hundred of the 135,000 evacuees will probably die as a direct result of Chernobyl radiation-induced cancer—an increase of a few percent over the number expected to die of cancer anyway. Worldwide, the spread of Chernobyl's radioactivity is likely to cause cancer fatalities, primarily in the northern hemisphere. As one major study concludes, "Most of the radiological impact is in Europe (including the European portion of the Soviet Union), which is projected to receive 97 percent of the collective dose commitment."[21] Eventually, Chernobyl will be responsible for about 17,000 excess cancer deaths in the European population, but the victims will be almost completely undetectable among the 113,000,000 cancer deaths expected in Europe during the generation after Chernobyl.

As uncertain as these lethality predictions are—they are based on limited fallout data and very limited biological effects data—the tendency has been to revise them upward. Recent studies of Hiroshima and Nagasaki survivors suggest that low levels of radiation may be far more lethal than previously thought. On the basis of these studies, a National Research Council panel recently concluded that Chernobyl's radiation-induced cancer fatalities could be four times higher than previously estimated.[22] The National Research Council's conclusions could also affect future Soviet decisions to evacuate people or to repopulate areas (assuming the Soviets agree with the Council's conclusions).

Soviet concurrence will be based, at least partly, on their firsthand experience with Chernobyl's survivors. Soviet citizens who were irradiated by Chernobyl's radioactive fallout comprise a grim peacetime analog to the Hiroshima and Nagasaki survivors. The Soviet medical establishment will track the medical experiences of hundreds of thousands of potentially irradiated people indefinitely, to understand better the potential long-term effects of low level radiation—primarily cancer and (possibly) genetic mutations.

Recovery Cost Estimates

The cost of the medical tracking and treatment program, along with other direct costs of the accident, including loss of the reactor, citizen relocations, and extensive decontamination programs, will be over four billion rubles (about seven billion dollars), if the most persistent cost estimates are correct. Indirect costs, such as power replacement, construction of new towns, and continuous radiation monitoring—both in and out of the Soviet Union—could more than double that estimate.[23] Entombment of the damaged reactor will incur continual expenses. Its sarcophagus is more than a passive concrete encasement. It contains a heat removal system to extract the heat created by radioactive wastes, as well as numerous embedded sensors to monitor the reactor's temperature and radioactivity levels for decades.[24] Evacuations and resettlements have also imposed continuous, as yet uncapped, costs. Over the past 4 years, the Soviets have discovered that the radioactive contamination was far more widespread than originally believed. Even now, Soviet authorities are planning future evacuations from parts of Belorussia.

The appendix shows a chronology of Chernobyl's cleanup cost estimates extracted from a variety of US and Soviet references, starting shortly after the accident in 1986 and ending in May 1990. The trend has been upward over time, as expected, but the chronology contains some interesting, discrete features (see the notes accompanying the chronology). For example, Belorussian resettlements 4 years after the accident account for the large step increases in July 1989 and April 1990 above the widely accepted figure of 8 billion rubles (about $13 billion).

The second graph in the appendix shows how all prior estimates pale in comparison to the two highest (April and May 1990) cleanup cost estimates. Soviet authorities developed those very high estimates apparently in an attempt to quantify the value of lost opportunities for production of electricity and agriculture. For perspective, the entire Soviet gross national product (GNP) in 1989 was about $2,142 billion, so the highest cleanup estimate, $415 billion, would constitute an immense portion of an entire year's Soviet economic output—19 percent of the GNP.

Estimating the cost of the accident is obviously as difficult and as inexact as estimating its radiological consequences (although the two are certainly related). However, the cost estimate trend has been unmistakable as time has passed. As knowledge of the accident's effects has increased, so have estimates of the cost to recover from it.

Some of those costs have been and will be borne by other countries. Practically every country in the northern hemisphere took some action to protect itself after Chernobyl. Most just monitored their air, water, vegetation, and livestock for signs of Chernobyl's contamination. Several European countries actually banned the export or import of foods that were at all likely to be contaminated, drawing angry protests from the Soviet Union. Two weeks after the start of the accident, the Soviet news agency Tass (in Kiev, capital of the Ukraine) reflected curiously mixed emotions of propagandized dismay over Western precautions and self-righteous concern for self-contamination:

> The Kiev bazaar today is leading its usual, bustling life. And this is while the West is proclaiming that the markets are closed in the Ukrainian capital and the stores are empty. . . . Contrived pretexts are being used as an excuse to ban exports of foodstuffs from the socialist countries. . . . Necessary precautionary measures have of course been taken to guard against the danger of the contamination of foodstuffs by radioactive substances. Radiation monitoring posts have been set up at the markets. . . . All foodstuffs and even flowers are tested for radiation before they are admitted to the trade hall. . . . As a precaution, the sale of milk, cottage cheese and sour cream has been halted at the markets. Green vegetables—onions, parsley, sorrel and spinach—are not being sold either.[25]

Postwar Comparisons

As pervasive and problematic as Chernobyl's fallout effects have been, they would certainly pale in comparison to the hypothetical effects of a nuclear war. The Soviets are most sensitive to that fact, and various Soviet writers have stressed that point since the accident. However, Chernobyl's radioactive fallout is different from nuclear weapon fallout. In his book describing the mostly futile attempts to save some of Chernobyl's early victims with bone marrow transplants, Dr. Robert Peter Gale declares that the Chernobyl accident released more radioactivity than the Hiroshima or Nagasaki bombs. His estimate generally corroborates a popular Soviet rumor that Chernobyl's explosion was "equal to three bombs of the type exploded at Hiroshima."[26]

In part, the basis for his claim is that the reactor's core contained more long-lived radioactive elements (by-products of uranium fissions) than would be created by a nuclear explosion. US scientists have estimated that the Chernobyl accident released 10 to 17 percent of the cesium-137 (a particularly long-lived radionuclide) released by *all* the atmospheric nuclear weapon tests combined.[27] Over many years, people exposed to radioactivity from the reactor accident would absorb more radiation than if they had been exposed to the relatively shorter-lived radioactive weapon debris. However, the total amount of radioactivity released initially by the accident was far less than even one modern weapon would release. The Soviets estimated that over the course of the 10 days it took to stop Chernobyl's radioactive emissions, the total radioactivity from all gases and particles released to the environment was less than 1 percent of the total radioactivity that would initially be created by a modern nuclear weapon.[28]

Even without a nuclear explosion (remember, the explosions were caused by steam and hydrogen—the radioactive contamination came from the pulverization and dispersal of waste elements in the reactor's core), Chernobyl was a disaster of truly unexpected and unprecedented proportions. Accident control and subsequent cleanup continue to stress large segments of the medical, construction, transportation, food distribution, and other infrastructures of Soviet society. Those stresses are evident in surprisingly frank Soviet press accounts of the cleanup process that is still going on today. Actually, the current Soviet openness in dealing with Chernobyl evolved only after clumsy, mercifully short-lived attempts first to deny the accident's existence, then to minimize the world's perception of its scope and widespread, lingering effects.

2. *The Strained Evolution of* Glasnost

PREDICTABLY, the Soviet government and press initially did their best to deny the accident's existence. After the initial coverup failed, Soviet leaders tried to minimize the damage to public opinion by implying that the accident was less severe than it really was, and that more terrible disasters have happened and continue to happen in the West. Too many Soviet citizens were affected, however, and rumors (some promulgated by the Western press) spread misinformation, fear, and panic in and out of the Soviet Union. The Soviets blamed the West, particularly the American government, for instigating yet another anti-Communist propaganda campaign, plotted around the Chernobyl accident.

Eventually, the Soviets came around, and in an unprecedented display of candor, let the world in on all the details of the accident, the response, and the clean-up efforts. The strained evolution of the Soviet government's *glasnost* about Chernobyl began 2 days after the start of the accident—after the cloud had drifted across Soviet borders all the way to Sweden. Finland actually detected Chernobyl's cloud a day earlier, but neglected to inform neighboring countries. The Swedish government boldly confronted Soviet officials with undeniable evidence that Sweden was being polluted by a radioactive cloud that had to have originated from within Soviet borders. After Sweden acted, the Kremlin reacted.

Sweden's Action

Chernobyl's radioactive smoke plume drifted initially to the north-northwest from the Ukraine, over the Belorussian Republic (figure 3), through Poland, the Baltics, Finland, and into Sweden. The cloud probably crossed Sweden's border Sunday afternoon, 27 April, more than a day and a half after the start of the accident. The radioactivity was detected early the next day by a laboratory at Studsvik, on Sweden's Baltic coast and at the Forsmark nuclear power station, 100 kilometers north of Stockholm.[1] The Studsvik laboratory and the Forsmark nuclear power station used air samplers and sensitive radiation detectors to monitor the radioactivity levels in the atmosphere, in the buildings, and on employees. Instruments measured personal radioactivity of employees as they arrived for work (to obtain a reference reading), and again as they left work (to detect any radioactive elements that may have been picked up on the job).

Early Monday morning, 28 April, Studsvik's unmanned air samplers were collecting particles with radioactivity levels that were as high as 30 times normal. In addition, laboratory and plant workers were *arriving* with radioactive contamination on their cars and clothes. Automatically assuming that their power station had problems, Swedish authorities evacuated the Forsmark plant. When they checked Sweden's other nuclear power stations and

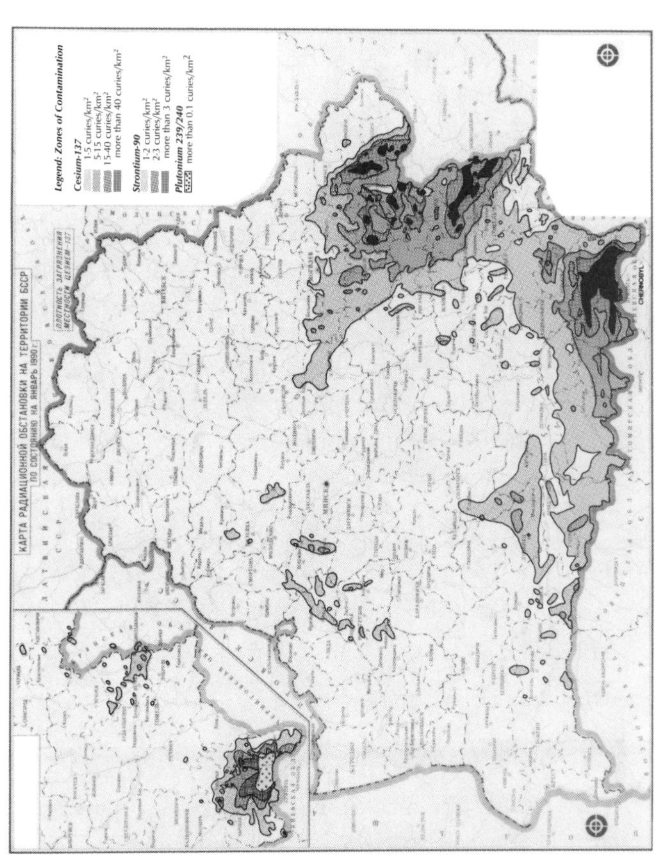

FIGURE 3.—*Area of radioactive smoke drift in the Belorussian Republic*

atmospheric monitoring stations, they discovered that much of the country had been blanketed with radioactive contamination. Radioactivity levels in some places were 100 times higher than normal.[2] Analyzing atmospheric dust samples, Swedish scientists confirmed that the radionuclides were coming from a nuclear reactor, not a leaking underground weapon test. Backtracking with recorded wind data (and technical assistance from US scientists), they deduced that a nuclear power plant accident had occurred somewhere in the Soviet Ukraine. Around noon on Monday (the accident happened on the previous Saturday), Swedish diplomats in Moscow presented their case to their Soviet counterparts and asked for information. Soviet officials simply said nothing.

The Kremlin's Reaction

Later that evening, at 9:02 p.m., almost 3 days after the initial explosions, a Soviet television news reader delivered the following announcement to the Soviet people:

> An accident has occurred at the Chernobyl Nuclear Power Plant as one of the reactors was damaged. Measures are being taken to eliminate the consequences of the accident. Aid is being given to those affected. A government commission has been set up.[3]

By then, at least two people had already died, several firefighters were dying, tens of thousands had been evacuated from Pripyat, and evacuations were still going on. The graphite fire was not yet smothered, and its radioactive smoke plume was sweeping toward the European mainland.

The Soviet government issued that announcement, tardy and terse as it was, because other nations were persistently asking for explanations. Several nations had collected irrefutable evidence that they were being contaminated with radioactive dust coming from a nuclear reactor inside Soviet borders. The announcement's terseness was in character: a kneejerk reaction by a Communist-controlled press that was long accustomed to keeping the masses underinformed. The announcement's tardiness was rationalized: Moscow officials simply may not have *known* the true extent of the accident. Furthermore, they may have been lied to by the onsite officials who *did* know and who were trying to avoid being the messengers of catastrophic information. In particular, some Ukrainians blamed Vladimir Shcherbitsky, the former head of the Ukrainian Communist Party, for covering up the events, for restraining the press, and for arresting dissidents after the accident.[4]

One analysis of Soviet press reports during the first week of the accident argues that the Kremlin was actually trying to deal with the disaster with a spirit of openness, but Ukrainian politicians betrayed Moscow by lying about the accident, trying to conceal its extent as well as their ineptness in dealing with it:

> For about 10 days after the accident, officials in Moscow were desperately trying to tell the world the truth as they knew it, but all the time were

> inadvertently relaying misinformation. The blame for this has been fixed on the officials on the spot, with possible further reprimands and dismissals gradually making their way up the Ukrainian party and state hierarchy . . . responsibility at Chernobyl, at least for the post-disaster chaos, has been laid by Moscow at the door of the Ukrainians.[5]

Not everyone agreed with that apology for the Kremlin's actions. Viktor Haynes and Marko Bojcun, experts on Soviet Ukrainian affairs, pointed out that the Soviet government commission took control as soon as they arrived at Chernobyl, less than 48 hours after the explosions. The assumption of authority entailed an assumption of responsibility:

> Except for the first day of the accident before its commission arrived in Pripyat, the blame for not giving radiation warnings on time and failing to take appropriate action has to be laid at the feet of the Gorbachev government. Republican officials can only be blamed for faithfully carrying out the centre's orders.[6]

The Soviet press printed details of the reactor explosion and fire for the first time on May 6, 10 days after the accident started. Even then, *Pravda* wove the facts into a tapestry of criticism for Western "rumor mongering" and praise for the firefighters and others (notably, Communist Party members) who were trying to control the situation.[7] Gorbachev's program of *glasnost* certainly wasn't instantly embraced by everyone involved with the Chernobyl accident.

Rumors

Rumors were a special problem in the Ukrainian capital, Kiev. Soviet authorities wanted to prevent the spread of fear and panic in that city of two million people, so they took extraordinary measures to keep Kievans in the dark. For example, the bus drivers who were sent from Kiev to evacuate Pripyat on Sunday, 27 April, had to sign oaths of silence.[8] Four days later, generally uninformed of the ongoing disaster less than 100 miles north, Kiev citizens celebrated May Day with parades and outdoor festivities. A political commentary in *Pravda* tried to use the May Day celebrations as real evidence that life was normal and safe in Kiev:

> On the evening of May 1, American and West European television networks were compelled to show shots from Kiev and Minsk, which up to that point had been depicted on those networks as cities that had suffered from the consequences of the accident in Chernobyl. Stunned Americans saw that mass holiday demonstrations were taking place there.[9]

Americans probably were stunned, but not for the reasons that Soviet propagandists thought. Admittedly, Kiev's May Day celebrants seemed unconcerned about the Chernobyl accident. Perhaps they appeared to be unconcerned not because they were convinced they were safe, but simply because they were uninformed. In the words of David R. Marples, a noted expert on the Ukraine and Soviet nuclear power who penned one of the first Western chronicles of Chernobyl's tragic events, the whole May Day scene in Kiev was a "surrealistic charade."[10]

It must have been hard *not* to wonder what was going on in the midst of bus caravans, arriving evacuees, hospitals filling up (with both radiation victims and radiophobic victims who ascribed any and all symptoms to radiation sickness), street and building washings, contamination checks at markets, and manpower mobilization for assistance at Chernobyl. *Glasnost* was slow to arrive. The initial lack of information and abundance of disinformation, coupled with the fact that thousands of citizens were being affected, naturally gave rise to speculation and rumor—inside and outside the Soviet Union.

Like the majority of Kievans who lacked first-hand information, the Western media initially based their reports about the accident on rumors, many of which were spread by travellers who left the Soviet Union shortly after the accident. Broadcast and print media also reported the opinions of self-proclaimed experts who had no more data than the press did. As a result, the initial Western media accounts of the Chernobyl accident were tainted with sensational, unverifiable allegations, including reports that thousands of people had died in the initial explosions, and a report that tens of thousands of victims had been buried in a combination mass grave/nuclear waste pit.[11]

In a study of the way the media handled the Chernobyl story in the Communist bloc nations, Radio Free Europe's researchers interviewed 3,788 East European nationals. Those interviewed—

Czechoslovaks, Hungarians, Poles, Romanians, and Bulgarians—were asked whether they had heard about Chernobyl, if so, how, and what they thought of the way the Soviets and their countries had handled the story. The study revealed that nearly half of all East Europeans who had even heard about the Chernobyl accident first heard about it on Western radio.[12] The overwhelming majority of interviewees expressed disappointment with their country's (and the Soviets') handling of the accident's information dissemination. Hungarian and Polish media coverage of Chernobyl didn't start until after the brief Soviet admission on 28 April, two days after the start of the accident. Bulgarian and Romanian coverage started on the 29th. Still, many interviewees echoed the Soviets' expressed disgust with perceived Western rumor mongering. One Ukrainian blue collar worker lamented: "Instead of spreading propaganda against us, the Americans, who have a lot of experience with leaks from nuclear power plants, could have helped us out."[13]

The Americans certainly could have helped, and they were prepared to do so. However, the Kremlin rejected President Reagan's offer to send a team of experts, including health physicists, medical technicians, and decontamination specialists. Soviet President Gorbachev did accept Armand Hammer's offer to send Dr. Robert Gale, a bone marrow transplant specialist, to help treat the most severe cases of radiation sickness. Dr. Gale's presence and assistance, however, didn't soften Soviet criticism of what they perceived as the West's amoral, opportunistic coverage of the Chernobyl accident.

Soviet Resentment

Gorbachev himself angrily denounced the tone and content of Western media reports. In a televised speech to the Soviet people, he expressed deep resentment over the apparent glee with which the Soviet disaster was met by his ideological foes:

> But one cannot ignore, cannot fail to give a political assessment of the way the event at Chernobyl was greeted by governments, political leaders and the mass news media in certain NATO countries, especially the U.S. They launched an unbridled anti-Soviet campaign . . . words about "thousands of casualties," "common graves for the dead," "the extinction of Kiev," the allegation that "all the Ukraine's soil has been poisoned," etc., etc. . . In general, we encountered a real conglomeration of lies—very shameless and malignant lies. . . . Its organizers, of course, were not interested in true information about the accident or in the fate of people in Chernobyl, in the Ukraine, in Belorussia, in any other place or any other country. They needed a pretext to defame the Soviet Union and its foreign policy, to weaken the influence of the Soviet proposals on ending nuclear tests and on eliminating nuclear weapons . . . to sow new seeds of distrust and suspicion of the socialist countries.[14]

Gorbachev went on to claim that the West's clamor for more information was politically motivated. To support his argument, he said that: "American authorities waited ten days to tell Congress and several months to tell the world about the Three Mile Island accident in 1979."[15]

What Gorbachev didn't explain in his speech to the Soviet people was that the US government was never *expected* to break the Three Mile Island news story. Facts and warnings were publicized instantly by plant personnel and the media. The ironic truth is that news of the Three Mile Island accident actually appeared in the Soviet newspaper Izvestia within 2 days after the accident.[16] Gorbachev's implication of a US coverup is belied by the dates on the Soviets' own newspaper articles about the Three Mile Island accident.

Damage Limitation

The Soviet media embellished Gorbachev's theme with a flurry of awkward, transparent attempts at "spin control" for damage limitation. On 6 May, *Pravda* told its readers that the Americans were using Chernobyl to whip up an anti-Soviet furor:

> to divert attention from criminal, aggressive actions by the U.S., like the recent bombing of Libya and the undeclared wars against Afghanistan, Angola and Nicaragua, and to justify a step-up in the arms race, the continuation of nuclear tests, and a refusal to accept Soviet peace initiatives.[17]

The Soviet press also published several old news stories about Three Mile Island and other non-Soviet disasters. In May and June, Soviet newspapers rediscovered not only Three Mile Island,[18] but also the Challenger shuttle disaster,[19] the grounding of "an American atomic submarine during combat patrol",[20] "another" accident at the Nevada underground nuclear test site,[21] "20,000 accidents and problems" at American nuclear power plants,[22] the Karen Silkwood story,[23] and problems at one West German[24] and two British nuclear power stations, one of which happened more than 25 years before.[25] *Pravda* hypocritically mused, "What can be more shameful than gloating over a misfortune?"[26]

Retrospectively, that early Soviet damage control propaganda reads like satire. The Soviets must have believed that the stories would protect their public image and that of their nuclear power industry. Recall that in 1986, they were aggressively modernizing the power industry in the Ukraine and other republics, dutifully executing Lenin's dictate to electrify the entire Soviet Union:

> Communism is the Soviet power plus the electrification of the whole country. . . . Only when the country has been electrified . . . only then shall we be finally victorious. . . . We must see to it that every factory and every electric power station shall become a center of enlightenment, and if Russia becomes covered by a dense network of electric power stations and powerful technical installations, our Communist economic development will become a model for a future socialist Europe and Asia.[27]

Protecting Nuclear Power

Protection of the nuclear power industry's image was clearly tantamount in the early days of the accident. Even before the graphite fire was smothered, Soviet authorities staunchly defended their nuclear power program. Boris Yeltsin, then a Politburo candidate, told German Communists on 4 May that the cleanup was progressing and that the Soviet government's energy program would persist in its efforts to exploit the atom for peaceful purposes.

That exploitation entailed risks. Failures and accidents were to be expected in fledgling, pioneering technologies like nuclear energy. On 7 May 1986, *Pravda* asserted, "trailblazers' paths are always thorny. Neither the pole, space orbits, atomic energy nor the ocean depths are subdued without tragic losses."[28]

Such fatalism was not sufficient to exonerate the nuclear power industry. The industry's image could theoretically recover faster if citizens perceived that at least some of the tragic losses were avoidable, caused by human error. Soviet authorities were quick to recognize the complicity of human errors and to punish those responsible, hoping to restore some confidence in the industry. During a 3-week trial, the power station's former director, its chief engineer (neither of whom was at the plant when the accident happened), and four others were convicted of ineptitude, indecisiveness, failure to observe procedures, and generally creating the conditions that led to the accident. The defendants argued unsuccessfully that the reactor design also contributed to the accident, but the

Soviets delayed investigations of reactor design deficiencies until long after human error had been blamed for the Chernobyl accident.

The Soviets weren't alone in their attempt to limit the damage to the power industry's image. Just 37 days after the Chernobyl explosions (less than a month after the graphite fire had been smothered), Dr. Hans Blix, head of the International Atomic Energy Agency, told attendees at the European Nuclear Conference that the nuclear power industry, like other indispensable human endeavors, would not be stopped:

> The Bhopal disaster, with some 2,000 deaths, did not stop the chemical industry; it is not possible. And the Challenger catastrophe is not stopping the U.S. shuttle program—whether indispensable or not. Nuclear power responds to very real needs and will also not be stopped.[29]

Unstoppable as it may be, the power industry also sensed that it had to distance itself from the anti-nuclear war sentiments born of the Chernobyl disaster. Traditionally, the world nuclear power industry has labored to separate itself from the military nuclear community in the public's eye, despite the fact that they share some materials, technology, and waste handling/disposal problems.

Association with nuclear weapons contributes to nuclear power's "dread factor": the perception that power plants deal with radioactivity, which is felt to be remote, mysterious, and capable of killing by itself or by inducing future cancers and mutations.[30] So it was not too surprising when a noted Western nuclear power expert, advocate, and Soviet nuclear industry watchdog insisted that the Chernobyl accident was *not* a preview of some of the effects of a nuclear war.[31] He declared that it was simply the obvious: a world-scale power industry accident that could be traced to deficient Soviet technology and operator error. On the other extreme, Dr. Robert Peter Gale, the American physician who worked with the Soviets by trying to save victims of severe radiation sickness, didn't hesitate to couple the Chernobyl experience with fearful expectations of the effects of nuclear war. In his book describing his medical assistance to Chernobyl's victims, Dr. Gale extrapolates:

> We've been dealing with a relatively small accident and, even with international cooperation, our ability to respond and care for the wounded has been limited. If we have a difficult time in helping three hundred victims, it's obvious that any response to the use of nuclear weapons will be inadequate. People who believe meaningful medical assistance is possible for the victims of nuclear war are mistaken.[32]

Interestingly, the Soviets themselves linked the reactor accident with the effects of nuclear war. They responded with military troops who were trained and equipped for operations in a radioactive battlefield. Furthermore, after the accident, Soviet officials repeatedly emphasized how their experience with Chernobyl had underscored the futility of nuclear warfare. Even the plans for an official Moscow cemetery monument to honor Chernobyl's dead heroes evidences nuclear power's "dread factor": the monument bears a symbol of the mushroom cloud that is commonly associated with an atmospheric nuclear weapon burst. Admittedly, the Soviets' linkage of Chernobyl to the horrors of war was also aimed at the West, where nuclear disarmament and anti-nuclear power sentiments have coalesced. The Soviets must have believed that their own industry would be relatively insensitive to linkage propaganda.

The Soviets had planned for their nuclear power industry to skyrocket in the 1990s. They, along with their European allies, were going to build two-thirds of the *world's* nuclear power capacity by 1995, increasing Soviet nuclear power output by 300 percent over an 8-year span. The plan was ambitious; even before Chernobyl, construction problems caused them to fall short of their scheduled goals. Not one of the seven Soviet nuclear power plants scheduled for startup in 1986 did.[33] The Soviets were determined not to let Chernobyl's events interfere with the long-term plan, however unrealistic.

Nevertheless, Chernobyl did affect the Soviet nuclear power industry and its plans. For example, the Soviets cancelled plans to construct two more reactors in addition to the original four at the Chernobyl complex. Nearly 2 years after the accident, every operating nuclear power plant and even those under construction were receiving bitter vocal opposition from local residents. Soviet citizens' protests caused authorities to scuttle plans for new power stations near Minsk, the capital of Belorussia, and Odessa on the Black Sea. Further, protests caused officials to halt the construction of a new nuclear power plant at Krasnodar (also near the Black Sea), where the Soviet government had already invested about 41 million dollars.[34]

Although Chernobyl's effect on the Soviet power industry has been relatively small compared to Three Mile Island's effect on the American industry, it has been remarkably persistent. That effect has flourished mostly because the Soviet government eventually did come forth with facts. Their unprecedented *glasnost* and tolerance of self-criticism has led to the development and expression of indigenous anti-nuclear public opinion. It has also supported restructuring (*perestroika*) in their nuclear industry's bureaucracy. The Soviet nuclear energy establishment is working closely with the US Nuclear Regulatory Commission to develop a system of legal and procedural controls for their infrastructure. Furthermore, their newfound willingness to cooperate internationally with agencies like the International Atomic Energy Agency suggests an abandonment of their isolationist "go it alone" attitude toward what the Soviets describe as a risky technological undertaking that is capable of affecting the rest of the world.[35]

The accident did affect much of the world. It directly touched the lives of hundreds of thousands of Soviet citizens, and it probably influenced the way millions of Soviets think about nuclear energy—and nuclear war. Today, Soviet citizens can express their opinions more freely than at any time since the Bolshevik revolution. If *perestroika* alters the Soviet political system to be more responsive to public opinion, then the Soviets' experience with the Chernobyl accident may very well influence official Soviet policies and attitudes about nuclear war.

3. Openness and Soviet Attitudes

THE SOVIET GOVERNMENT'S initial lack of openness and responsiveness was quite consistent with the traditional lack of importance of public opinion in policymaking. However, in 1986, that was starting to change. Gorbachev was beginning his attempt to restructure Soviet society, in part by encouraging *glasnost,* openness in dealing with problems. The Chernobyl accident became an instant and historic opportunity, both for openness and for the formation and tolerance of diverse public opinion. If Gorbachev's reforms ultimately succeed, public policy formulation could actually embrace that public opinion.

The Chernobyl accident had an indelible effect on the opinions and actions of Soviet citizens because it influenced so many people's attitudes toward government, nuclear technology, and nuclear war. Attitudes were affected because lives were affected in numbers far beyond those who experienced the evacuations, the radiation sickness, the mobilizations for accident control and cleanup, and the precautions to limit the spread of radioactive elements. More than five million people (almost two million of them children) had to take stable (nonradioactive) iodine supplements as a precaution, saturating their thyroid glands to prevent Chernobyl's radioactive iodine from concentrating in their bodies.[1] Soviet *Pravda* correspondent Boris

Oleinik described how widely felt the accident was in the Soviet Union:

> What happened at the Chernobyl Atomic Power Station . . . has brought pain to the hearts of more than just the local population. It has touched the heart of every Soviet person. . . . No matter whom you talked to, you sensed their anxiety [caused by] uncertainty, which was contributed to sometimes by delays in information about the real state of affairs at the accident site.[2]

The Soviet people *know* they were kept in the dark by their government, and many citizens, Ukrainians especially, resent the rapid pace of nuclear electrification in their land. Furthermore, the accident fueled the nuclear power industry's "dread factor": the linking of peaceful, beneficial power technology to the potential effects of a nuclear war.

Many of Chernobyl's horrors were recorded vividly by Soviet author Grigoriy Medvedev in his notebook of interviews with eye witnesses and participants, including some who were terminally ill with radiation sickness. Academician Valerii Legasov's memoirs (published after his suicide) also contain firsthand accounts of the accident. They illustrate how his attitude—that of a respected Soviet scientist and nuclear power advocate—changed after the accident. Even Soviet President Gorbachev cited Chernobyl when he linked the lessons learned from the accident to the perceived horrors of nuclear war.

Perestroika *and Chernobyl*

Gorbachev highlighted that link and explained what he believed to be Chernobyl's lesson in his book about Soviet new thinking and societal restructuring, *Perestroika.* In it, he declared that the Soviet Union has succeeded "in containing the consequences of the accident . . . the situation is under control. . . . Those to blame for the catastrophe have already been brought to trial."[3] The sole lesson he cited was that the atom, even the peaceful atom, can be dangerous when it gets out of control. He concluded his discussion of Chernobyl by reverting to castigation of the West for spreading what he perceived as malevolent, malicious lies about the accident.

Although his book is intended for Western readers, it is clear he is trying to convince his own people, as well, of their government's earnestness in dealing with the aftermath of the Chernobyl disaster. After his ascension to power in 1985, Gorbachev preached that *glasnost,* openness in treating the Soviet society's pervasive problems, is absolutely necessary for the success of his restructuring efforts. Chernobyl was a litmus test for *glasnost.* The accident affected so many people, inside and outside the Soviet Union, that its story, like its radioactive cloud, simply could not be contained.

Gorbachev's declaration of Chernobyl's lessons was significant not just because it linked the accident with nuclear war (for obvious propaganda benefit in the West), but also because his statements were laced with self-congratulatory expositions of how *open* the Soviet government has been, and continues to be, about the disaster:

> We were responsible for both the evaluation of the accident and for the right conclusions. Our work is open to the whole nation and to the whole world. . . . There must be full and unbiased information about what happened.[4]

Notably absent from *Perestroika* was any mention of the role that deficiencies in Soviet nuclear power technology may have played in causing the accident. Western analysts, the US Nuclear Regulatory Commission (NRC) in particular, have pointed to reactor and safety system design deficiencies as culprits:

> Nuclear design, shutdown margin, containment, and operational controls at U.S. reactors protect them against a combination of lapses such as those experienced at Chernobyl. . . . Assessments in the light of Chernobyl have indicated that the causes of the accident have been largely anticipated and accommodated for in commercial U.S. reactor designs.[5]

Watershed at Vienna

The NRC's assessments were facilitated by the Soviets' release of information about the reactor's design, its performance, and the actions of operators just before the accident happened. Much of that information came from Soviet officials at the International Atomic Energy Agency's Vienna meetings, first convened in late August 1986 to explain the

Chernobyl accident to the world. That Vienna meeting was a watershed for Western analysts, a milestone in the evolution of Soviet *glasnost.*

Soviet government officials and scientists went to the meeting armed with data and information about the accident's sequence, radioactive fallout intensities, population protection measures, and the Chernobyl reactor design. Some of the attendees, an assortment of about 500 engineers, scientists and nuclear experts from outside the Soviet Union, complained, predictably and justifiably, that the Soviet exposition was simply inadequate to judge the true extent of risks and environmental insults from the accident. Vienna was just a start—it must have been anathema for Soviet officials, long accustomed to secrecy in such matters, to open up as much as they did, then and later. The president of the US National Council on Radiation Protection and Measurements described data in the Soviet Vienna report as "better than we had a right to expect."[6]

The further release of information about Chernobyl eventually permitted independent analysts to judge for themselves how the accident happened. The government's eventual openness (still incomplete in the minds of many Western analysts) also provided insights into the way the government and the Soviet press handled the whole affair from the outset. As a result, the Soviet people *know* that their government underinformed them during the days immediately after the accident. Citizens have openly criticized their government's actions—their words reflecting lingering attitudes of distrust toward government technocrats, whom they perceive as responsible for causing the accident, covering it up, then perpetuating risky technological endeavors after the accident without informed popular support.

An unfortunate legacy of the Soviet bureaucracy's initial coverup attempt was the absence of documentary films depicting the early stages of the accident, evacuations, relocations, and efforts to snuff the graphite fire. The USSR State Cinematography Committee denied Russian and Ukrainian filmmakers' requests to go to Chernobyl for documentary coverage. One Soviet *Pravda* reporter complained,

> Bureaucrats from the filmmaking department preferred to sit on the sidelines and do nothing to let the country and the world find out the truth about the events in Chernobyl . . . for 20 days not one movie cameraman shot any footage at the station or around it.[7]

Moviemakers simply echoed the criticisms of Soviet citizens and reform-minded officials. In the weeks and months after Chernobyl, they frequently cited the need for more honesty and openness in dealing with the Chernobyl accident and the cleanup efforts.

The government's long-range cleanup campaign has continued to be a target of criticism. Many local residents complained of flagrant safety violations during the cleanup and construction of the sarcophagus built to seal the damaged reactor. Others complained that officials failed to take their health concerns seriously. Sufferers were called "radiophobic" for blaming radioactive contamination for both real and imagined aches and pains. One theme is common: citizens felt betrayed, stonewalled by the government organizations entrusted with responsibility to protect them.

David R. Marples agreed. Analyzing Soviet and Polish press reports from the early days of the accident, Marples discovered that Soviet nuclear experts had briefed Polish officials and helped them establish a disaster response plan for Poland. From the dates of the announced meetings and activities, Marples deduced that the Soviets had discussed plans for Poland's population and environment protection from Chernobyl's radiation, while simultaneously feeding its own citizens political statements, mostly indignation over the West's apparently insensitive reaction.[8]

Others didn't see the Soviets' response in Eastern Europe as much more humane than their treatment of their own people. European nuclear disarmament advocate Mark Thompson quoted a Polish underground newspaper to remind the world that initial notification of the Chernobyl accident was neither timely nor firsthand from the Soviets:

> The Chernobyl tragedy has once again shown Moscow's astounding arrogance toward its satellite countries. The Polish authorities found out about it from a Tass communique when the radioactive cloud was already over Poland. Soviet experts who arrived in Warsaw did not bring any concrete facts but only came to measure radiation levels in Poland.[9]

Press censorship (including collusion in the Kremlin's attempted coverup) and government actions certainly limited the Soviet citizens' and the world's knowledge and understanding of what happened during the early stages of the accident. Facts have escaped, though, because so many people were affected. In particular, survivors, workers, and eyewitnesses comprise a valuable source of information for understanding how the accident affected attitudes.

Witnesses and Victims

In his "Chernobyl Notebook," a piece that might have forced his exile had it been written before the more tolerant days of *glasnost,* Grigoriy Medvedev reviewed the accident and its causes through the testimony of people who lived the events. Medvedev is a nuclear technology expert and advocate, but he apparently didn't let expertise influence objectivity in his Chernobyl report. He vigorously supported Gorbachev's call for *perestroika* by highlighting the incompetence and irresponsibility that he perceived led to the accident. Medvedev essentially blamed the Soviet government's Ministry of Power Industry and Electrification for the initial Chernobyl coverup attempt; it was they who fostered secrecy to the point that nuclear power facilities weren't sharing knowledge about even routine breakdowns and environmental impacts. The industry was incapable of building an open experience base, learning from mistakes and problems as it matured.

One tragic manifestation of such negligence was the primitive level of accident prevention and reaction training. That lack of training may have contributed to suffering and deaths among Chernobyl's first wave of firefighters. Medvedev's account includes the story of two junior "practitioners" who worked for Chernobyl's senior reactor control engineer. The two men were sent to observe the extent of the wreckage with their own eyes soon after the explosions:

> Wearing no masks or protective clothing, they entered the reactor hall littered with burned wreckage. They saw the fire hose pouring water at the reactor. The water came out but there were no longer people. The firemen had retreated several minutes earlier, . . . Taking good mental note of all they had seen, Proskuryakov and Kudryavtsev spent no more than a minute near the reactor. This was enough for them to absorb a lethal dose of radiation (both died in terrible pain at the 6th Moscow clinic).[10]

Medvedev's notebook frankly personalizes the Chernobyl story in a way that no previous Soviet disaster could have been described to its citizens. Tales of the evacuations, the firefights, the livestock slaughters, and citizens' expressions of frustration and resignation animate the tragic events. Pripyat's evacuees were told to pack lightly; they'd be back in about 3 days. Local militia men weren't evacuated; they relieved the firefighters shortly after the explosions. Like the two young "practitioners" sent to scout the burning reactor core, militia men wore no protective clothing. They didn't even have radiation dosimeters to monitor their exposure. Medvedev's account includes testimony describing soldiers picking up radioactive shrapnel, pieces of the reactor's fuel rods, and chunks of graphite core with their bare hands.

Medvedev interviewed several of the gravely ill patients who had been evacuated to a Moscow hostital for specialized care. He found some victims agonizing over the cause of the accident nearly as much as the pain from their burns and radiation sickness. Men died after considerable suffering and elaborate but futile attempts to treat them with blood transfusions and bone marrow transplants. The most radioactive corpses had to be buried in zinc caskets to retard the return of their bodies' radioactive contamination to the earth's crust.[11] V. G. Smagin, the damaged reactor's shift chief, recounted the heroic actions of the plant's operators who died trying to bring the reactor under control. Smagin also explained to Medvedev how the accident had affected his attitude.

> The earth was blocked from doing its final work, that of turning the bodies of the dead into dust. Accursed nuclear century! Even here, in the age old end of man, tradition thousands of years old was being violated. It was impossible even to give the people to the earth. . . . Your death woke up the people, pulled them out of blind dull obedience.[12]

"Out of blind dull obedience"

Academician Valerii Legasov was the deputy director of Moscow's Kurchatov Atomic Energy Institute and a member of the commission assigned to control the accident and clean up activities. He also headed the Soviet contingent to the Vienna meetings. Legasov was predictably quick to defend publicly the Soviet nuclear power industry. Less than 6 weeks after the start of the accident, Legasov told a *Pravda* interviewer that nuclear power stations were at the "pinnacle" of engineering achievements; they were economically and ecologically sensible. To Legasov, the very future of civilization was "unthinkable without the peaceful use of atomic energy."[13] A year later, Legasov insisted that the Chernobyl accident was not about to alter the course of the Soviet Union's agressive nuclear electrification plans. They would certainly learn from the Chernobyl experience—safety would be stressed more—but modernization would continue. Besides, in historical perspective, Chernobyl was not "the most terrible" accident in terms of human losses.[14]

Legasov committed suicide on 27 April 1988, 2 years almost to the day after the start of the Chernobyl accident. In his posthumously published memoirs, Legasov focused on the "blind dull obedience" of the Soviet nuclear reactor community on safety issues. He blamed the current generation of Soviet engineers for not thinking more critically about their jobs and about safety in general. He concluded that the accident was the "apotheosis and culmination of all the improper management

. . . that had been going on in our country for many decades."[15] However, unlike earlier investigators who tried and punished plant managers and operators for the accident, Legasov indicted the technology, the reactor safety control systems in particular, for contributing to the accident, concluding, "when one considered the whole chain of circumstances, the mistakes and attitudes which surrounded the accident, it was impossible to point to one particular person or decision as the guilty party or the cause of the disaster."[16]

The absence of a single, identifiable, readily understandable cause for the accident made it even harder for citizens to accept the official line of logic: progress entails risks; the risk is small but finite, so accidents happen; worse accidents have happened; benefits still outweigh risks—so trust the government and scientists, and press on. For many Soviet citizens, the accident's effects were unacceptably intrusive, too severe to continue accepting the risk/benefit equation of the government's nuclear electrification program. Aleksandr Levada, a 20-year resident of Pripyat, explained how the Chernobyl accident affected his attitude:

> Science must do its utmost to see that the energy of the atom, upon being "unchained," never again gets out of control. The tactless attempt to apply the formula "science demands sacrifice" to the Chernobyl anomaly must be rejected out of hand. Scientists have sometimes risked their own lives in experiments, injecting themselves with plague microbes, for example, and mankind bows to their

> heroism. But true scientists have never extended this risk to other people.[17]

Legasov substantiated that risk by asserting that a similarly devastating accident *could* happen again at any of the other Soviet reactors like Chernobyl. He feared that history could repeat itself.

Nuclear Test Site Change

It is precisely that fear that has affected Soviet peoples' attitudes toward their nuclear industries. The accident and the cleanup efforts (along with no small amount of international pressure) convinced the Soviets to stop building Chernobyl-type reactors and to tighten the safety controls and operational procedures on the ones that are still in use. The chairman of the USSR State Committee of the Utilization of Atomic Energy summarized how much the accident affected their nuclear industry:

> It may seem strange to claim that one major accident has influenced the development of the entire nuclear power industry, but it is so. Chernobyl required such great efforts from the national economy when it came to eliminating the consequences of the accident, so shook the public, and showed up so clearly many shortcomings in the nuclear power industry that for a long time yet it will be the starting point for the adoption of many decisions.[18]

The same apprehension that affected policy in the power industry has affected the nuclear weapon development industry. For example, neighbors of the Soviet Union's favored underground nuclear test site, Semipalatinsk, have convinced the Supreme Soviet legislature that testing should be stopped there. Concerned about the potentially hazardous effects of radioactive gases that frequently leak from underground nuclear weapon tests, local residents vehemently and successfully argued that the Semipalatinsk test site should be abandoned. Future weapon tests will be done at an alternate, remote Arctic test area. The Soviet Academy of Medical Sciences reinforced citizens' fears by attributing a variety of maladies among local residents (including cancer and a high infant-mortality rate) to radioactivity from atmospheric nuclear weapon tests that were conducted more than a quarter of a century ago.

Realistically, though, the Soviets probably had many reasons for stopping weapon tests at Semipalatinsk. However, the Kremlin's decision to stop testing there comes after "the unexpectedly swift development of a powerful grass-roots movement, reported to involve hundreds of thousands of citizens"—real evidence of the "widespread apprehension among the Soviet populace about radiation dangers" after Chernobyl.[19] Thus, the disaster created public alarm, which led to government actions, and those actions will actually influence the effectiveness of nuclear forces.

Debate: Stronger or Weaker Deterrence?

Soviet force effectiveness certainly shapes the US deterrence-based strategy, but deterrence remains an attitude of fear—fear of reprisal. However, the thought processes that produce that fear may not even be coherent. Steven Kull, a Stanford University Research Fellow and professional psychologist, interviewed several US and Soviet defense policy-makers, trying to understand the psychological processes they used to formulate deterrence policy. The interviews revealed patterns of what he diagnosed as inconsistent and incoherent logic. Kull blamed the reality of dealing with nuclear weapons for the way defense planners think:

> I do not see defense planners as necessarily having coherent conceptual and attitudinal frameworks in their approach to defense issues. In general, people are not consistent . . . the apparent inconsistencies in military thinking are at least partially derived from the complexities of adapting to the new conditions engendered by nuclear weapons.[20]

The Chernobyl accident may have added to those complexities and produced a new set of inconsistencies. Did the recovery experience make the Soviets more fearful of nuclear war, or did it enhance their confidence in the ability to recover from it? Those questions underlie a debate about whether the accident's consequences will ultimately hinder or promote the deterrence of nuclear war.

Soviet civil defense is at the heart of the debate. Civil defense is a much greater factor in Soviet defense policy formulation than it is in its US counterpart. For years, Western analysts have interpreted Soviet war survival preparations as a sure sign that they were preparing to "fight and win" a nuclear war. The Chernobyl accident was a practical test for their civil defense system. They learned much about its effectiveness from the cleanup and recovery process. If the Soviets use their knowledge and experience from Chernobyl to fortify their civil defense system, then Chernobyl may actually have weakened deterrence. The accident may provide strength and confidence in the Soviet system charged with orchestrating their society's survival in a nuclear war. Could confidence in survival actually weaken deterrence?

4. Weaker Deterrence

IN A WAY, Chernobyl actually did weaken deterrence. The accident forced the Soviets to learn how to deal with some of nuclear war's most feared collateral effects. They could exploit the knowledge that they derive from their experience: they could use it to prepare more effectively for nuclear war fighting and recovery. Preparation dispels fear. If Chernobyl improves Soviet readiness for nuclear war, it could reduce their fear of it. Improved planning could reduce the Soviets' perceptions of the risks associated with conflict escalation, at least to limited nuclear confrontation.

The Soviet civil defense infrastructure would have to play a key role in much of that planning. The Soviets believe that they must convince their enemies that their nuclear strength is credible in order to deter nuclear war. That credibility hinges on their enemies' belief that the Soviets could (and would, if necessary) use nuclear weapons—without committing suicide from an enemy's retaliation. In other words, they must be able to "rationally threaten to resort to [nuclear] war."[1] The "rational" quality of such a threat is based on their perceived ability to survive retaliatory nuclear attacks, to rebuild industrial and social infrastructures, and to govern surviving citizens. Civil defense is supposed to manage all that. On a comparatively small scale, Chernobyl tested the Soviet civil defense system.

The system did not respond as well as expected. Even so, Chernobyl's lessons certainly haven't been lost or ignored by Soviet military planners.

Soviet Civil Defense

For years, Western analysts have credited the Soviets with an extensive and presumably highly effective civil defense system. That system was very much responsible for the popular, widespread perception that the Soviet Union was preparing to "fight and win" a nuclear war.[2] Soviet civil defense was a nationwide organization of more than 100,000 full time workers controlled by the military. The system has cost them about $20 billion over the last 20 years, mostly for equipment, training, shelters, and industrial hardening.[3] At least 70 percent of Soviet industrial workers (about 30 million civilians) belong to some sort of civil defense organization. The military civil defense force works with the civilians. Military members train to do many rescue and damage-limiting operations, including firefighting, first aid, and the detection and monitoring of radioactivity, chemicals, and biological agents. (The Soviet civil defense organization must also handle natural disasters.)

Their system has three objectives. First, it must protect people: leadership, essential workers, and everyone else—in that order of priority. Second, it must protect and restore, if necessary, Soviet factories and other centers of productivity. Third, it must assist survivors with postwar recovery.[4] Toward those objectives, the Soviets have built numerous shelters; they have developed evacuation plans—including relocation plans for much of their essential workforce; and they have trained citizens to administer first aid, decontaminate living areas, and restore power in emergencies. US analyses of Soviet civil defense effectiveness suggest that successful execution of their evacuation plans alone could reduce nuclear war casualties by 50 percent.[5] Unquestionably, the evacuations from Chernobyl saved lives.

Soviet civil defense planning is comprehensive and even more impressive when compared to US civil defense. Perhaps reflecting a sense of futility with respect to "fighting and winning" a nuclear war, the US system is a scrawny, underfunded, and underequipped planning shell. The US system is voluntary at the state level. It does not maintain a large standing force, civilian or military. Including part-timers, US emergency management people number about 7,500. US civil defense doesn't discriminate in its evacuation plans, maintaining no provisions for identifying, much less protecting, key industries or their workers. US fallout shelters are unstocked and located mostly in large cities, where they are at risk of destruction. The US has no nationwide evacuation plan; states do it voluntarily and some have opted not to do it at all. The US civil defense system costs about 60 cents a year per citizen. The Soviet system costs them more than $14 a year per citizen.

The relatively high cost and priority of civil defense in the Soviet Union imply correspondingly high expectations for its effectiveness. However, Soviet literature makes it clear that the system didn't quite meet expectations even under Chernobyl's comparatively benign stress.[6] For whatever reasons—incomplete mobilization, bureaucratic inertia, confusion (the "fog of war"?)—Soviet civil defense at Chernobyl didn't perform as expected by Soviets *or* by Western Sovietologists.

Test Failure at Chernobyl

In his analysis of the systemic factors that contributed to the Chernobyl accident, the University of California's Professor William C. Potter says that Soviet Civil Defense literally failed the test posed by Chernobyl.

> Performance of Civil Defense units was unsatisfactory and was hindered by poor training, understaffing, ineffectual equipment, and a convoluted command structure that was unresponsive to rapidly changing crisis developments . . . the typical, pre-Chernobyl, Western image of a massive, well-equipped, finely tuned, and vigilant Soviet Civil Defense apparatus corresponds poorly to the actual conduct of Civil Defense forces prior to and in the immediate aftermath of the Chernobyl accident.[7]

Professor Potter further observes that no Civil Defense personnel received awards for their performance at Chernobyl, and the Military Chief of Soviet Civil Defense lost his job.

In a display of *glasnost* nearly 2 years after the accident, the Ukraine's Civil Defense Staff Chief, Lieutenant General N. Bondarchuk, discussed his organization's shortcomings. He pointed to the lack of training, both practical and psychological, in emergency response actions. He even referred to the existing training procedures, drills, and exercises as shams. Soviet civil defense officials were simply unable to comprehend the gravity of the situation, to make intelligent decisions, and to direct subordinates.[8] He blamed poor civil defense publicity and public training for the citizens' ignorance of how to avoid contact with radioactive fallout, how to evacuate, and how to protect food and water from contamination.

Of course, even if the public *had* been educated, it would have done little good during early hours when radiation levels were probably highest, because radiation reconnaissance was neither timely nor complete. Firemen, police, and even radiation monitoring specialists lacked the equipment and training necessary to gather data required to measure and map the radioactive environment. Furthermore, civil defense evacuation plans were developed on the wartime premise that evacuations would be from urban to rural areas, not from rural to urban for medical support and housing. Bondarchuk elaborated on those shortcomings in the emergency plans:

> They did not consider that the rise of extensive zones of contamination could necessitate the evacuation of the rural inhabitants. The CD [civil defense] plans which were worked out did not clearly reflect the questions of determining the dispersion areas, supporting the evacuation, safeguarding the housing abandoned by the residents as well as the personal property of the citizens or providing transport to

> evacuate livestock . . . they did not consider the particular features of the radiation situation in an emergency at an AES [atomic energy station], the organizational forms for medical aid to the public were not completely thought out, and there was no provision for iodine prophylaxis and antiradiation agents.[9]

Actually, Chernobyl can't be considered an objective test of the Soviet civil defense system. The system's inability to cope with the rural reactor accident at least suggests that the thrust of Soviet civil defense preparations have been for war recovery. The absence of emergency preparations was also a manifestation of blind faith in Soviet nuclear technology. Popular literature (e.g., *Soviet Life* magazine) propagandized that faith, but as previously noted, Valerii Legasov lived long enough to condemn the complacency that such propaganda and blind faith produced among Chernobyl's workers.

Self-Criticism and System Improvements

The Soviets have been surprisingly frank with self-criticism of the civil defense system's response at Chernobyl. They have learned from their mistakes, and are using their knowledge to restructure the system. Civil defense authorities are determined to learn from Chernobyl, in order to improve the system.

For example, the deputy chief of civil defense for the entire Soviet Union called for better training through more realistic exercises and site drills. Referring directly to Chernobyl, he insisted that civil defense leaders show initiative and creativity when developing and testing plans for warning systems, field radioactivity measurements, decontamination, population evacuation, and medical assistance.[10]

A new civil defense training program has been designed for vocational and high schools. Training has been extended to the general population through the use of revamped mass media courses and training films. A year after Chernobyl, a teacher at a Moscow art institute described how civil defense training is now conducted for her fellow teachers:

> Every month, a serious elderly man—a Civil Defense instructor—comes to our institute. Taking up half of our working day he tells us about defense measures in case of a nuclear explosion, using as visual aids, booklets and illustrations yellowish and worn out with use.[11]

The Soviets have done more than training and education. Less than 2 years after the Chernobyl accident, Soviet literature boasted of an impressive variety of technological innovations that were developed to enhance the effectiveness of civil defense. They have developed lightweight synthetic materials for anti-radiation suits, an electrically charged paint that repels dust particles, and new surfactants (soaps) that are effective in cold water as cleaning agents for decontamination washes.[12]

The Soviets have also developed new medical supplies to enhance their effectiveness in treating victims. Prostheses, tapes that would replace sutures, and synthetic glues to repair bone fractures and broken blood vessels are examples. They even claim to have developed three revolutionary "designer" drugs that literally flush radioactive substances from the human body. As described in *Izvestia* in 1988:

> They are the first special-purpose drugs in radiology. One is obtained from an animal gland, and two are synthetic. Their purpose is to promote the rapid excretion of radioactive matter from the body. They are not tablets or powder. The drugs will be added to bread and meat products. Initial tests have shown that they accelerate the body's radiological "mine sweeping" by almost twenty- or thirty-fold.[13]

To be accepted by the general population, though, the new drugs may have to compete with Chernobyl's popular "decontamination cocktails." Following the accident, Soviet civil defense officials had to deal with persistent rumors that alcohol, red wine, and vodka especially, offered some protection against the effects of radiation. A concoction of iodine-laced vodka was rumored to be a particularly effective radiation antidote. There was even a rumor that the evacuation bus drivers had been *issued* a special cabernet wine to accompany their vodka (allegedly sold at cut-rate prices to affected residents) to combat radiation effects. The local militia chief, General A.I. Ivashchenko, unequivocally refuted such rumors by announcing: "all of the cock-and-bull stories about alcohol's supposed beneficial effect against radiation are a patent fabrication."[14] The alcoholic remedies seem even more ridiculous considering how advanced Soviet radiation medicine was advertised to be.

Actually, Soviet medical scientists may have some justifiable confidence in their ability to diagnose and treat some effects of nuclear radiation. If, as some speculate, several accidents have actually preceded Chernobyl with widespread radioactive contamination, then Soviet researchers could have already capitalized on them the same way they have at Chernobyl. For example, Soviet scientists had almost 30 years to draw lessons from an accident at the Kyshtym nuclear waste storage facility. Kyshtym's chemical explosion probably contaminated a larger area and killed more people than the Chernobyl accident. As reported in *Pravda,* "The Kyshtym accident may have assisted subsequent preparations by emergency services of fire, health and militia."[15]

Soviet secretiveness or confidence in their recovery capabilities may both have played a part in their initial refusal to accept medical assistance from other countries, notably, the assistance of American bone marrow transplant specialist Dr. Robert Peter Gale. They eventually did invite Dr. Gale to help treat the most severely radiated victims, and he was quite impressed by their sophisticated methods.

The Soviets downplayed the need for and effectiveness of Gale's work compared to their own techniques. Upon learning that American doctors were coming to help, patients were quoted by the Soviet news agency, Izvestia, as saying: "Well, let them come. After all, they have to learn, too."[16] Soviet doctors made it clear that the treatment processes were well underway by the time Gale and colleagues got there, and that Soviet doctors were always in the driver's seat.

> His [Dr. Gale's] coming was important and productive. Our colleagues participated in the work correctly and respectfully. We also had some differences of opinion, naturally. And then we did what we ouselves thought necessary. When we argued, Prof. Gale would say: "Stop! End the discussion. We'll do what our hosts tell us." Most likely, we would behave the same way in his clinic.[17]

The assistant director of the Belorussian Academy of Sciences' Biophysics Institute later attacked Gale after he [Gale] publicly estimated that, by the turn of the century, several thousand people could be dead from the long-term effects of Chernobyl's widespread radiation:

> I know Gale. I confess I was very surprised to hear such a statement from that scientist and physician. No country's scientists have experimental data showing that small doses of radiation cause anemic, oncological or any other changes in the human body. For the residents of Khoiniki [a Belorussian town downwind of Chernobyl] and other districts adjacent to the 30-km [kilometer] zone, there will be no aftereffects.[18]

Predicting the effects of low-level radiation is a controversial art. However, based on the Chernobyl data collected for the past 4 years and analyses of nuclear bomb survivor data, world scientific opinion appears to be overwhelmingly on Gale's side.[19] Also, Khoiniki is still so contaminated with Chernobyl's fallout that residents are protesting Moscow's imposition of farm production goals, saying that agricultural products from their soil would be unsafe for consumption. More than 4 *years* after the accident, the Supreme Soviet approved money for the future resettlement of up to 200,000 more people who have been living in contaminated areas. Current analyses of radioactive fallout data and biomedical effects, along with opinions of international organizations, are compelling the Soviets to consider more precautions, as they attempt to contain and reduce the accident's effects.

New data, materials, and medicines weren't the only improvements to the Soviet civil defense system that were spurred on by Chernobyl. Soviet chemists have developed ways to reduce the effects of radioactive contamination on crops. The Soviets claim that soil liming can reduce plant uptake of the fallout radionuclide strontium-90 (28-year half-life) by as much as a factor of five. Soviet research also indicates that nitrogen fertilizers can reduce plant uptake of both strontium-90 and cesium-137, another long-lived fallout radionuclide (30-year half-life), by an order of magnitude: a factor of *10* reduction.[20]

Reducing radioactivity was also the goal of Soviet livestock studies. Three years after the accident, their research produced practical, effective ways to reduce or eliminate contamination in animals. Feed grain protection, dosimetry testing, and feed rationing methods are all parts of a comprehensive new plan to ensure that meat is safe to eat even after a nuclear war. Chernobyl offered some very specific lessons:

> Chernobyl confirmed that when making up rations for various groups of livestock, it is necessary to allow for the following: dairy cows and pregnant livestock should be fed primarily grain, coarse feeds of herbaceous crops, corn, and potatoes. Rations should not include the tops of root-bearing plants, since they contain an increased amount of strontium-90. It is necessary to increase the amount of mineral additives containing potassium and calcium.[21]

Post-Chernobyl livestock research has also produced specific feed recipes to reduce dairy cattle's uptake of strontium-90. Soviet scientists have used data from the farms around Chernobyl to identify permissible levels of grass contamination for unrestricted cattle grazing, and a threshhold body contamination level for livestock, above which veterinary treatment would be required. They expect that such newfound knowledge derived from the Chernobyl accident will permit them to increase production of safe meat products in contaminated environments.

In addition to the livestock, medical, and vegetation studies that the accident either spawned or encouraged, Chernobyl also revealed that the bureaucracy entrusted with the war-survival mission needed reform. Civil defense authorities studied and upgraded several operational aspects of their system. They were ready with improved operational techniques less than a year after the Chernobyl accident. As an example, the Soviets folded Chernobyl's lessons into a civil defense exercise at a meat processing combine. They wanted to test the effectiveness of civil defense planning and worker training. The civil defense chief in charge of the exercise related it to Chernobyl:

> Considering that our exercise took place some time after the accident at the Chernobylskaya AES (Chernobyl Atomic Electric Power Station), we intensified political indoctrination and explanatory work, which allowed each person to perceive the need for Civil Defense more objectively. For example, after deepening their knowledge and skills in using dosimetric instruments in city CD courses, personnel of the RKhN (radiation and chemical observation) post themselves became good instructors . . . people had an opportunity to measure for themselves the radiation level, become convinced of the total safety and tell colleagues about the actual state of affairs.
>
> After the comprehensive exercise we decided to use the radiation-proof shelter as a CD classroom. . . . Thus by coming here combine personnel also become familiar with materials revealing the essence of CD measures.[22]

The local military chief of civil defense commended the meat combine's civil defense director for the quality of the training exercise, noting that the exercise benefitted from the hard work of a variety of organizations. In particular, he cited the

Communist Party members, the trade union, and the local Young Communist club. A high-ranking Communist Party official seconded the civil defense chief's praise, and he related the exercise to the real thing; he praised the exercise as "an advance payment for the future."[23] Thus, the Soviets not only learned ways to improve their chances of surviving a nuclear war, but they also applied the knowledge by integrating and testing it.

The Soviets were quick to assimilate Chernobyl's lessons and convert them into survival skills. One apparent reason for such promptness was their disappointment with the civil defense system's response under fire. As with any failed bureaucracy, "heads rolled" and swift, effective repairs were encouraged and rewarded by the government. In their rationale for improving civil defense, Soviet analysts frequently cited the obvious: the need to protect citizens from the effects of nuclear weapons and nuclear power plant accidents. The Soviets also pointed to one not-so-obvious excuse for improving civil defense: to protect citizens from *conventional* weapon attacks on nuclear power installations.

Targeting Reactors

Perhaps revealing some new, post-Chernobyl targeting philosophies, Soviet analysts have openly discussed the potential vulnerability of the West's reactors to attack by conventional weapons. Conjecturing that recovery from a reactor attack would be like recovery from nuclear war, the Soviets hypothesized that attacking reactors could have potential military value. They could produce the effects of nuclear war without using a single nuclear weapon:

> For example, in Western Europe, which is full of chemical plants, petroleum refineries, and atomic and other power stations, even a conventional conflict would bring destruction fully comparable to the consequences of nuclear war. It is obvious that the same situation also exists in other parts of the European continent and in North America and Japan.[24]

Even Soviet President Gorbachev commented on the potential vulnerability of nuclear reactors in Europe. Less than 3 months after the Chernobyl fire was extinguished, in a speech to French President Mitterrand, Gorbachev said,

> Nuclear war is not the only thing that poses a mortal danger. There are more than 150 atomic reactors and hundreds of chemical plants on European territory. Only a few conventional artillery shells are enough to destroy a reactor and take many human lives. In any variant, conventional or nonconventional, an armed conflict would detonate a world catastrophe.[25]

Gorbachev's prediction makes it clear that the Soviets know that they have the option to target reactors, or threaten to do so, if they ever think it is in their national interest. Apparently, the Chernobyl experience wasn't difficult, dangerous, or expensive enough to preclude Soviet military assessment of the value of damaged nuclear reactors on enemy territory. Threatening to "create Chernobyls" could be part of a plan to control the escalation process during a conflict. With reactors as targets, Soviet war planners may not need as many nuclear weapons as they have today for either deterrence or warfighting. In the future, if the Soviets take steps to lessen their own vulnerability to reactor attacks, like hardening or burying reactors, then Chernobyl would indeed have taught a lesson that weakened deterrence.[26]

Chernobyl has already taught the Soviet Union many potentially valuable lessons about nuclear war survival and postwar recovery. They learned that their civil defense bureaucracy was ineffective, and they learned how to correct many of its defects. They developed and tested plans for protecting people, livestock, and crops from the effects of radioactive fallout. Furthermore, Chernobyl added momentum to their already vigorous research and development of special materials, medicines, and decontamination techniques. At a minimum, "With Chernobyl, the Soviets have consolidated a research advantage on the post-attack recovery period."[27] Chernobyl strengthened the Soviet civil defense system and, in a way, may have reduced some uncertainties, some fears of using nuclear weapons. If it did, it weakened deterrence.

Unquestionably, Chernobyl also made the Soviets more sensitive to the potential effects of nuclear weapons, and the effects of conventional weapons on nuclear power stations. Fortunately, Soviet literature also points to the "down side" of targeting reactors: they *also* rely heavily on nuclear power (many of their reactors don't even have containment vessels). Thus, the Soviets themselves are particularly vulnerable to reactor attacks. They know it. They also know how agonizing and expensive the Chernobyl cleanup has been. Those lessons were extraordinarily painful and personal. Thus Chernobyl probably strengthened deterrence more than it weakened it.

5. Stronger Deterrence

SOVIET LITERATURE offers abundant evidence that Chernobyl really did make the use of nuclear weapons less acceptable to a lot of people. The accident taught the Soviets that they were far less prepared than they (or anyone else, for that matter) thought they were to "fight and win" a nuclear battle. The physical cleanup and medical aspects alone have been unimaginably difficult, time consuming, and expensive. Four years after the accident, the Soviets were still trying to "eliminate the consequences" as they put it, and they are doing so with unprecedented levels of international assistance. Interdependence is insurance against the reversibility of *glasnost.*

The Soviets have shared fallout, medical, and reactor design information with the West more openly than ever.[1] Information sharing along with some aggressive investigative reporting by Soviet writers reveal that Chernobyl has very much strengthened the deterrence of nuclear war. Even the deterrence-weakening military lesson—reactor targeting with conventional weapons—is a two-edged sword. The Soviet Union is as vulnerable as the West is, and they know it. Their recognition of that potential vulnerability may have motivated the Soviets to finally ratify a Geneva Protocol that outlaws nuclear reactor attacks.

The 1977 Geneva Protocol

The 1949 Geneva Conference produced a new Convention forbidding acts of war that could jeopardize civilian populations. The 1977 Conference went even further in an attempt to balance military and humanitarian interests. It added two Protocols to the 1949 Convention, one of which specifically prohibits the destruction of installations that could produce widespread injury to the noncombatant population. Those installations include nuclear power plants. The Protocol doesn't even permit targeting *near* nuclear plants. Article 56 of the Protocol spells out the agreement, including the conditions for abrogation:

> Article 56. Protection of Works and Installations Containing Dangerous Forces
>
> 1. Works or installations containing dangerous forces, namely dams, dykes and nuclear electrical generating stations, shall not be made the object of attack, even where these objectives are military objectives, if such attack may cause the release of dangerous forces and consequent severe losses among the civilian population. Other military objectives located at or in the vicinity of these works or installations shall not be made the object of attack if such attack may cause the release of dangerous forces from the works or installations and consequent severe losses among the civilian population.
> 2. The special protection against attack provided by paragraph 1 shall cease:

(a) for a dam or a dyke only if it is used for other than its normal function and in regular, significant and direct support of military operations and if such attack is the only feasible way to terminate such support;

(b) for a nuclear electrical generating station only if it provides electric power in regular, significant and direct support of military operations and if such attack is the only feasible way to terminate such support;

(c) for other military objectives located at or in the vicinity of these works or installations only if they are used in regular, significant and direct support of military operations and if such attack is the only feasible way to terminate such support.

3. In all cases, the civilian population and individual civilians shall remain entitled to all the protection accorded them by international law, including the protection of the precautionary measures provided for in Article 57. If the protection ceases and any of the works, installations or military objectives mentioned in paragraph 1 is attacked, all practical precautions shall be taken to avoid the release of the dangerous forces.

4. It is prohibited to make any of the works, installations or military objectives mentioned in paragraph 1 the object of reprisals.

5. The Parties to the conflict shall endeavour to avoid locating any military objectives in the vicinity of the works or installations mentioned in paragraph 1. Nevertheless, installations erected for the sole purpose of defending the protected works or installations from attack are permissible

and shall not themselves be made the object of attack, provided that they are not used in hostilities except for defensive actions necessary to respond to attacks against the protected works or installations and that their armament is limited to weapons capable only of repelling hostile action against the protected works or installations.

6. The High Contracting Parties and the Parties to the conflict are urged to conclude further agreements among themselves to provide additional protection for objects containing dangerous forces.
7. In order to facilitate the identification of the objects protected by this article, the Parties to the conflict may mark them with a special sign consisting of a group of three bright orange circles placed on the same axis, as specified in Article 16 of Annex I to this Protocol. The absence of such marking in no way relieves any Party to the conflict of its obligations under this Article.[2]

Ratification After Chernobyl

The United States, the Soviet Union, and 100 other nations signed the Protocol in 1977. The Soviets didn't ratify it until 12 years later, 3 years after the Chernobyl accident. While the Soviets didn't explicitly relate ratification to Chernobyl, Soviet diplomat Igor Gavrichev explained that "We were hesitating [to ratify the Protocol], but Soviet policy is changing, including its humanitarian policy. The humanitarian component in Soviet foreign policy is growing, perhaps not as fast as we wish, but steadily."[3]

Soviet foreign policy's "humanitarian component" probably grew in direct proportion to the Soviets' realization of how devastating a damaged reactor could be, and how many nuclear power stations were operating on Soviet territory (there are about 50 nuclear power plants operating in the Soviet Union today).[4] Soviet ratification of the Protocol suggests that concerns for self-preservation and humanitarian interests at least coexist with interest in the military exploitation of reactor vulnerability. The West might never know whether ratification of the Protocol eliminated any existing Soviet plans for reactor targeting. A skeptic might conclude that 1) the Soviets ratified the Protocol in hopes of eliminating some of their own perceived vulnerability, while retaining the option to hold the West's plants at risk; and 2) it is inconceivable that a country without a viable legal system would even consider tactical restraints based on international agreements. Or, to paraphrase Cicero: "inter arma silent leges": the law is silent in time of war.[5]

The effectiveness of international legislation aside, the Soviets may have had another credible reason to ratify the Protocol: propaganda. The United States has not yet ratified it. US experts in international law basically objected to Article 56's lack of specificity: who would define "severe" population losses in paragraph 1 of the Article? Paragraph 2 permits attacks on power plants if they are used "in regular, significant and direct support of military operations." Modern electricity grids may integrate many power sources to support a variety of customers. Identifying the "military support" targets may be impossible. Finally, paragraph 5 outlaws the attack of plant defenses, possibly turning nuclear power facilities into "safe havens" for enemy forces.[6] The United States has less technical but probably more insurmountable objections to other articles in the Protocol. US specialists fear that some of the other Articles in the first Protocol could "legitimize terrorist activities of national liberation movements" by applying the humanitarian rules of *international* conflict to terrorist-combatants in *civil* conflicts.[7]

Apparently, the Soviets had no such objections to the Protocols. They either planned to ignore them anyway, or decided that they could live with the Articles as written. Perhaps the Soviets didn't review the Protocols' details with the tenacious pedantry of US legal scholars. It is interesting to note that all representatives to the Convention in 1977 agreed with the Protocols' wording. However, the timing of Soviet ratification strongly suggests that their experience with the Chernobyl accident cleanup may have motivated them to do everything they could to reduce the likelihood of having another blown-up reactor on their territory.

"A Sinister Game"

When Valerii Legasov told Belorussian writer Ales Adamovich that another reactor accident like Chernobyl *could* happen, he wasn't referring to an enemy's hostile action. However, the effect could be as devastating. Adamovich called for citizen involvement to help guide national energy policies. Involvement and commitment would also be necessary for an effective civil defense. Legasov also saw the need for public intervention:

> Another Chernobyl would be the downfall of restructuring [*perestroika*], and it would be followed by unforeseen social and world cataclysms. An exaggeration? No! The shocked numbness after the first Chernobyl is not likely to be repeated, nor is the large-scale heroism. We can expect instead an angry reaction: "What are they doing to us? How much do we have to take?" Our salvation requires drastic intervention by the public to stop this departmental madness, in which "the projects of the century" begin to resemble "the crimes of the century."[8]

When the Soviet government ratified the Protocols, the impact and extent of Chernobyl's radioactive contamination were still unfolding. Some investigative Soviet reporters who wrote about the cleanup were aware of their government's initial coverup attempts. The Soviet press reminded readers of the coverup, while exposing inequities in the recovery efforts and shortcomings in civil defense. Few writers shared the civil defense system's dispassionate desire to capitalize on Chernobyl's lessons in order to improve the chances of surviving a nuclear war. In fact, some questioned the system's effectiveness even *after* incorporating Chernobyl's lessons.

One Moscow resident called his organization's post-Chernobyl civil defense exercise a "sinister game without any rules whatsoever." He said that food- and water-stocked shelters were myths, and that the exercises made him "feel that war is sure to begin, that it cannot be avoided, that we should evacuate to somewhere completely defenseless and chaotic, it is as if we are talking about an archery competition, not atomic war."[9] The exercise was imperfect, like the actual cleanup and recovery process at Chernobyl.

Even so, the accident's cleanup and citizens' reactions were far more impressive and opinion forming than any sterile civil defense exercise. In reality, officials on the scene were indecisive, firefighters and cleanup crews were ill equipped (but truly heroic), citizen evacuations were delayed, looting was widespread, fire extinguishing required herculean efforts, radioactive contamination was (and still is) more widespread than initially thought, and sophisticated medical treatments proved to be largely ineffective. For all the political hoopla surrounding Dr. Gale's and other American physicians' contributions, the Soviets initially downplayed their value. At the Vienna meeting of world experts in August 1986, the Soviets reported that Gale's work with Chernobyl victims had shown that bone marrow transplants were useless for patients who had received high doses of radiation, and actually dangerous for others.[10]

Something must have changed their minds since then, however. In April 1990, the Soviets sent a radiation sickness patient with pre-leukemia symptoms to the United States for a bone marrow transplant. Anatoly Grishchenko had flown a helicopter over the reactor five times in 1986 to drop sand and other fire-smothering materials onto the burning graphite core. His helicopter had lead shielding, and he wore a lead-lined suit for protection from external radiation. Nevertheless, he was apparently sufficiently irradiated to induce cancer. Soviet doctors admitted that they could not help him, so their government agreed to pay the cost (about $150,000) for surgery in the United States. Unfortunately, the surgery could not save him; he died of cardiopulmonary failure 3 months later.[11]

Another example of the Soviet medical system's real, self-acknowledged limitations in dealing with radiation sickness was a recent hunger strike by 120 Chernobyl radiation sickness patients. They fasted "to protest inadequate medical care, including shortages of drugs and hospital beds . . . at the Institute of Medical Radiology" in Kharkov.[12] Most telling was the fact that this occurred more than 4 years after the Chernobyl accident.

Grishchenko's treatment and strikes by Chernobyl's victims hardly suggest that the Soviet medical establishment is anywhere near capable of successfully supporting national war survival and recovery efforts. If so, it means that many Soviets no longer believe that they could "fight and win" a nuclear war, if they ever really did. The alternative is prevention.

Lingering Fears

The lesson that prevention is the key was too widespread in the Soviet press to have been orchestrated solely by a Communist propaganda campaign. Certainly, early on, some politicians did try to use the accident's story to evoke anti-nuclear and pro-disarmament sentiment in the West in order to advance their own political agenda. However, as the scale of the Chernobyl disaster unfolded, and *glasnost* flourished in much of the Soviet press, the sincere desire to deter war, not to prepare for it, has spread. A year after the accident, Dr. Hans Blix, the Director-General of the International Atomic Energy Agency, actually credited Chernobyl with producing a "new way of thinking" in the Soviet government, and he encouraged the continued evolution of truthful press reporting.[13]

The accident made the thought of nuclear war unacceptable to a lot of people who were either not asked or not permitted to express themselves before Chernobyl's *glasnost* permitted freer expression. In a 1987 article about new power plant safety measures, an Izvestia editor commented, "Before the Chernobyl misfortune, we did not have a very good idea of the damage that could be inflicted on nature and people by radioactivity gone out of control."[14]

Chernobyl's runaway fire had barely been extinguished when noted Soviet academician G. Arbatov declared "how irrational and absurd the very idea of a nuclear war is."[15] A month after the accident, the vice president of the USSR Academy of Sciences said, "Chernobyl warns us that we have experienced only a tiny incident compared to a thermonuclear catastrophe."[16] Academician Vladimir Sokolov concurred, adding an apocalyptic warning that: "the facts [about the accident and its aftereffects] illuminate the depths of the abyss that will yawn before mankind if preparations for a nuclear war are not halted."[17]

A Russian Orthodox Church official also related Chernobyl's lesson to the apocalypse. Responding to assertions that the Bible foretold the accident and its significance (remember, as discussed in chapter 1, *Chernobyl* is a translation of the word *wormwood,* the falling star of which is supposed to signal the end of the world), the Ukrainian Exarch explained that nuclear disarmament could delay the apocalypse indefinitely:

> Man cannot know the times foretold in the Apocalypse. . . . Atomic weapons exist, and in such numbers that they can blow up our earth. . . . If mankind obtains the proper level in the moral sense, it will not only not use nuclear weapons but will destroy them. In that way, what is written in the Apocalypse—that time—will be put off to an indefinite distance.[18]

Thus, in the minds of many Soviets, especially those millions who were directly and indirectly affected by the fallout, the lingering lesson of Chernobyl is fear: fear of nuclear war. That fear is compounded by deep distrust of national leaders and organizations—particularly the ones who tried to hide the accident, then failed to protect citizens and their families as the truth emerged. "People lost all faith in scientists, government officials and even their doctors."[19] Lacking that faith, and possessing such fear, citizens will insist on stronger deterrence. Stronger deterrence should logically translate into political moderation, international involvement, and support for arms reduction and nuclear nonproliferation agreements.

6. After Chernobyl

THE ACCIDENT and cleanup efforts occurred as historic changes were happening in the Soviet Union. More openness and societal restructuring with "new thinking" affected the way the Soviets handled the accident. And vice versa. Chernobyl fostered *glasnost,* becoming an early paradigm for *perestroika.* Either way, the disaster greatly affected millions of people's lives and attitudes. Chernobyl deeply influenced the way Soviet citizens think about their leaders and their society's vulnerabilities, and so it affected deterrence.

Soviet literature was never more "open." Political and military commentaries, along with stunningly frank investigative reports, suggested two competing conclusions about Chernobyl's effects on deterrence. Chernobyl strengthened deterrence and, at the same time, weakened it. The "weakened it" case is very real, but tenuous. To believe that deterrence was weakened, that Chernobyl made nuclear war *more* likely, is to believe that the Soviets learned enough about civil defense, decontamination, and war recovery to offset all the punishing lessons of the accident. They would have to be less fearful of using nuclear weapons than they were before the accident. What would be the source of such confidence? Did Chernobyl validate and improve their civil defense program? Did it revolutionize their technology for postwar recovery?

A Lack of Confidence

Chernobyl's lessons for improving civil defense sounded good, but reports about their practical implementations and practice exercises hardly inspired confidence. Many followers weren't convinced that the system was credible, and many leaders deserted their posts. Desertion was a popular option for a surprising number of officials. According to Viktor Haynes and Marko Bojcun, who wrote about people who were touched by the accident, Communist Party authorities couldn't find 177 of Pripyat's 2,611 Party members (540 of whom worked at the power station) during the accident's first week.[1] Many deserters were publicly accused of cowardice, then uncermoniously dumped from Party ranks.

Even the technological readiness gain, the "research advantage on the post-attack recovery period,"[2] is dubious. If they are so medically advanced, so self-sufficient that they could "fight and win" a war, why do they need, and continue to seek, outside help—several *years* after the accident? Most recently, the Belorussian government independently asked for foreign assistance in their efforts to clean up their land and evacuate their citizens. They have appealed directly to the International Atomic Energy Agency and to the United Nations for modern medical and radiometric equipment, diagnostic computers, medicines, resettlement support facilities, and transportation services for school children.[3]

Even if Chernobyl *had* given them new knowledge, they'd still need confidence in their political and military leadership. The *glasnost* generated by

Chernobyl, along with *perestroika* in their society (their nuclear industries, in particular), has done little to instill such confidence. How many Soviet citizens trust their decisionmakers, their nuclear experts in particular, more now than they did before Chernobyl? The accident, along with other *glasnost*-motivated revelations of nuclear crises like Kyshtym, Beloyarskaya (see chaper 4), and, of all things, the Cuban Missile Crisis, have reinforced citizens' distrust of decisionmakers. More than 3 years after the accident, Soviet writers condemned their government's "Big Lie" about Chernobyl:

> The lie did not begin now—it began three and a half years ago. I think that we still do not know the most essential truth about the accident.[4] . . . Now let's take a look at what the lie has turned into. It has turned into a big lie against the whole country . . . the people who are guilty of all these crimes, of all this lying and deceit, of concealing the truth—these people cannot change the situation. This is because, to cover up their lies, they will have to keep on dodging and lying.[5]

Soviet citizens simply can't trust the existing bureaucracies and government officials to get them out of the mess, because they got them into it in the first place, then lied about it. Soviet commentaries reach a logical conclusion: public interest should have been their government's first priority.

Soviet citizens know quite well that Chernobyl wasn't the first time that public interest took a back seat at the Kremlin. Three years into the Chernobyl cleanup, Soviet citizens learned about their leaders' actions in the Cuban Missile Crisis. There is an interesting parallel between public reactions to Chernobyl and reactions to revelations about the "Carribbean Crisis," as the Soviets refer to the Cuban Missile Crisis. In February 1989, Soviet political commentator Stanislav Kondrashov condemned government secrecy, and asserted that public policy should reflect the people's will:

> Placing missiles in Cuba was a Soviet idea . . . [the missiles] had been sent to Cuba secretly. . . . It was a well-kept secret, and, as is our custom, we continued to keep it from our own people even after others had exposed it. . . . Our whole people were brought to the edge of the nuclear abyss without knowing about it, without having the opportunity to understand why—for just what reason! . . . [It was] total disregard for their right to know things that pose the question of their life or death. . . . In 1962, Khrushchev was simply never confronted with the question of whether or not he or the other leaders of that time had the right to put the fate of their people at risk in order to aid another people, the Cubans. . . . Democracy is a complicated concept that is different for different countries, and especially for different systems, but any operating democracy—not one that is just for show—means a policy, domestic and foreign, that is attuned to the will of the people.[6]

"The Will of the People"

What is "the will of the people" after Chernobyl? Is it to improve their ability to "fight and win" a nuclear war, or to deter one? Overwhelming evidence in the Soviet press supports the latter. *Glasnost* has made it easier to know the people's will. The Soviet press is discussing both domestic and foreign policy issues with increasing candor. *Perestroika's* success will be measured by how much influence citizens actually have on future government policies and actions.[7] Democratization will surely help to inject the influence of millions of people whose attitudes were affected by Chernobyl.

Some popular influence might already exist. In addition to citizens, bureaucrats, and scientists, the Soviet military establishment has been deeply involved in recovery from the accident. Thousands of soldiers assisted with the cleanup. They included civil defense corps and chemical defense units, as well as air force, army, and reserve troops.[8] Unknown numbers of military people suffered and died as they performed assigned duties at Chernobyl. The head of the Soviet chemical defense troops, Colonel-General Pikalov, personally led repair crews through highly contaminated areas of the Chernobyl power station into the damaged reactor control room. He later recalled, "People went at the circumstances as though into battle."[9] He praised the valor of his men and cited Chernobyl's military lesson:

> Let's not neglect the military aspect. The Chernobyl accident is a drop in the ocean, compared with a nuclear bomb. Great is the responsibility of all states and people everywhere to avert the nuclear threat.[10]

If Pikalov and other military members really believe that, and if the military has any influence on the Soviet decisionmaking process, then the Soviet military might just be a source of moderation in future decisions that involve escalation of hostilities. They've been through it once; they should be less likely to recommend actions that would send them back. Chernobyl might have *already* influenced the attitudes of national command authorities.

Chernobyl's effects on deterrence are all perceptions of *intentions.* However, changed intentions really aren't sufficient to strengthen deterrence. Soviet *capabilities* to wage war also have to change, just in case their intentions also change. The United States should consider actions that substantiate Chernobyl's lessons by actually reducing Soviet capabilities to wage nuclear war.

Lessons for Deterrence

One of Chernobyl's most conspicuous lessons is that retaliatory forces don't have to contain gigatons of nuclear weapons in order to deter aggression. (In fact, they may not need *any,* if combatants ignore the Geneva Protocols and threaten to attack nuclear power plants.) The accident implied that the use of nuclear weapons could be more destructive and cause more persistent damage than previously thought. Furthermore, because defenses are imperfect at best, weapon use could even be self-destructive.

After Chernobyl, each weapon's deterrent value increased along with the Soviets' fear of suicide if they actually exercised a nuclear option. Therefore, significant reductions in nuclear arsenals should be more acceptable to them. Reductions should go all the way down to levels that cause their planners (and Western experts on Soviet defense) serious doubts whether the Soviets could "fight and win" a war or even coerce another nation.

However, the Soviets aren't likely to disarm below whatever level they feel supports their claim to superpower status. Given the present state of the Soviet economy, nuclear weapons may be their *only* claim to superpower status.

The Chernobyl experience gave the Soviets plenty of reasons, maybe even renewed their sense of urgency, to reduce nuclear forces and expand arms control agreements. To do either or both requires cooperation and a certain level of trust. Confidence-building measures are needed first. Interactions that lead to interdependence, such as help with the Chernobyl cleanup and transferring nuclear reactor safety technology, will foster some trust. That should take the inheritors of the Soviet nuclear arsenal one step closer to realizing the lessons that the rest of the world hoped they'd learn: the ones that will *strengthen* deterrence after Chernobyl.

Appendix: A Chronology of Recovery Cost Estimates

July 1986	A Soviet government commission investigated the causes of the Chernobyl accident and reported to the Politburo that direct losses would total about 2 billion rubles. See: "In the Politburo of the CPSU Central Committee," *Pravda,* 20 July 1986, 3. Translation in *The Current Digest of the Soviet Press* XXXVIII, no. 29: 1.
April 1987	Valerii Legasov, Deputy Director of Moscow's Kurchatov Institute of Atomic Energy, estimated that the direct cost of recovery from the Chernobyl accident would be 2 billion rubles. He defined direct costs as including the sarcophagus, decontamination efforts, new housing construction, and compensation payments to evacuees. He could not estimate the accident's additional, indirect costs such as the loss of electricity and farmland. See: Valreii Legasov, interviewed by Nikolai Vikhlyayev, *Novosti Press Agency,* April 1987. Translation published in *Bulletin of the Atomic Scientists* 43, no. 6 (July/August 1987): 33. The 2 billion ruble estimate was corroborated by the Soviet Union's Minister of Finance in Andrey Illesh,

	Chernobyl (New York, NY: Richardson & Steirman, 1987), 197.
July 1987	Chernobyl's costs include "agricultural and other economic losses *worldwide* that top $4.5 billion," according to Jeff Trimble, "The Lessons the Soviets Learned," *U.S. News and World Report,* 20 July 1987, 14.
January 1988	"The direct costs of eliminating the consequences of the accident came to about 4 billion rubles, and if losses attributable to reduced volumes of industrial production in these areas and other expenses are included, about 8 billion rubles." "In the Politburo of the CPSU Central Committee," *Pravda,* 15 January 1988, 1. Translation in *The Current Digest of the Soviet Press* XL, no. 2: 20.
May 1988	Science magazine cited Soviet sources (at a May 1988 Kiev conference on Chernobyl's medical effects) for their $15 billion estimate to recover from Chernobyl. Direct costs were 4 billion rubles, with a matching amount for indirect costs. They converted to dollars ($1.70 per ruble), and added $1.4 billion to account for other countries' costs in order to arrive at their 8.8 billion ruble ($15 billion) estimate. See: Lynn R. Anspaugh, Robert J. Catlin, and Marvin Goldman, "The Global Impact of the Chernobyl Reactor Accident," *Science* 242, no. 4885 (16 December 1988): 1518.

June 1988	Soviet academician Leonid Abalkin, Director of the Economics Institute of the USSR Academy of Sciences, estimated that Chernobyl's cost was 2 percent of the Soviet national economy: 11 billion rubles. *Tass,* 31 May 1988. Translation in *National Affairs* FBIS–SOV–88–107 (3 June 1988): 59.
September 1988	Professor A. Protsenko, Chairman of the USSR State Committee on the Use of Atomic Energy, tried to imply that Chernobyl's cleanup costs were *relatively* insignificant when compared to the cost of environmental repair from all industries and power facilities. He estimated that Chernobyl's cost was 8 billion rubles, but the environmental impact of all other Soviet technological endeavors was 50 billion rubles *per year.* See: A. Protsenko, "Atomic Power: After Chernobyl," *Pravda,* 6 September 1988, 3. Translation in *The Current Digest of the Soviet Press* XL, no. 36: 8.
April 1989	Three years after the accident, the *direct* loss estimate was 8 billion rubles, compared to 4 billion a year earlier. Indirect losses would add to that figure. See: N. Baklanov and A. Illesh, "At the Station, In the Zone and Nearby," *Izvestia,* 26 April 1989, 6. Translation in *The Current Digest of the Soviet Press* XLI, no. 18: 27.
July 1989	The Soviet Belorussian republic received about two-thirds of all the contamination from Chernobyl in the Soviet

Union. Sensing that the Kremlin's financial relief plan slighted them, Belorussian Deputies to the Supreme Soviet told Moscow that they needed more relief money to pay for evacuating 106,000 more residents (vice Moscow's estimate of 11,000). On top of the prevailing recovery estimate of 8 billion rubles, the total became 18 billion rubles. See: "Who'll Pay the Bill for Chernobyl?" *Pravda,* 30 July 1989, 3. Translation in *The Current Digest of the Soviet Press* XLI, no. 30: 35. *The New York Times* (Francis X. Clines, "Soviet Villages Voice Fears on Chernobyl," 31 July 1989, A3) reported the Belorussian request as 16 billion dollars, implying an exchange ratio of 1.6 dollars per ruble. That ratio converts all estimates in this table except where conversions were provided in the reference.

April 1990 — In April 1990, the Supreme Soviet approved a $26 billion program for additional resettlements. That is on top of the popular estimate of $12.8 billion (8 billion rubles) to pay for recovery. See: Elizabeth Shogran, "A Year Later, Chernobyl's Ills Widen," *Washington Post,* 27 April 1990, A1, A36. (See figure A–1, this section, April 1990 bar).

April 1990 — Four years after the accident, Time magazine cited "a Soviet government institute" estimate that the cost of Chernobyl's cleanup, including the value of lost farmland and production, could go up to $358 billion. See: Anastasia Toufexis, "Legacy of a Disaster," *Time* 135, no. 15 (9 April 1990): 68. (See figure A–1, this section, April 1990 bar).

May 1990 — *Newsweek* followed suit by quoting Ukrainian Soviet Deputy Yuri Shcherbak's upper bound estimate of $415 billion as the ultimate cost of Chernobyl's cleanup. See: Carroll Bogert, "Chernobyl's Legacy," *Newsweek,* 7 May 1990, 31.

To appreciate the magnitudes of the last two estimates, it is interesting to compare them to an entire year's gross national product (GNP). The US Central Intelligence Agency estimated that the 1989 Soviet GNP was about $2,142 billion. The Chairman of the Council of Economic Advisors, Michael Jay Baskin, said that the CIA estimate was too high. He put the 1989 Soviet GNP at about $1470 billion. Viktor Belkin, a prominent Soviet economist, was even more pessimistic than Baskin; he said that the 1989 Soviet GNP was about $1,176 billion. Even over that wide range of estimates, Chernobyl's highest recovery cost estimate would constitute a very large portion—19 percent to 35 percent—of their GNP. Of course, the Soviets (and others) will spread Chernobyl's cleanup costs over the many years that will be required for recovery. This comparison is made only to provide a perspective on the cost estimates. Michael Wines reported the Soviet GNP figures in "C.I.A. Accused of Overestimating Soviet Economy," *New York Times,* 23 July 1990, 6.

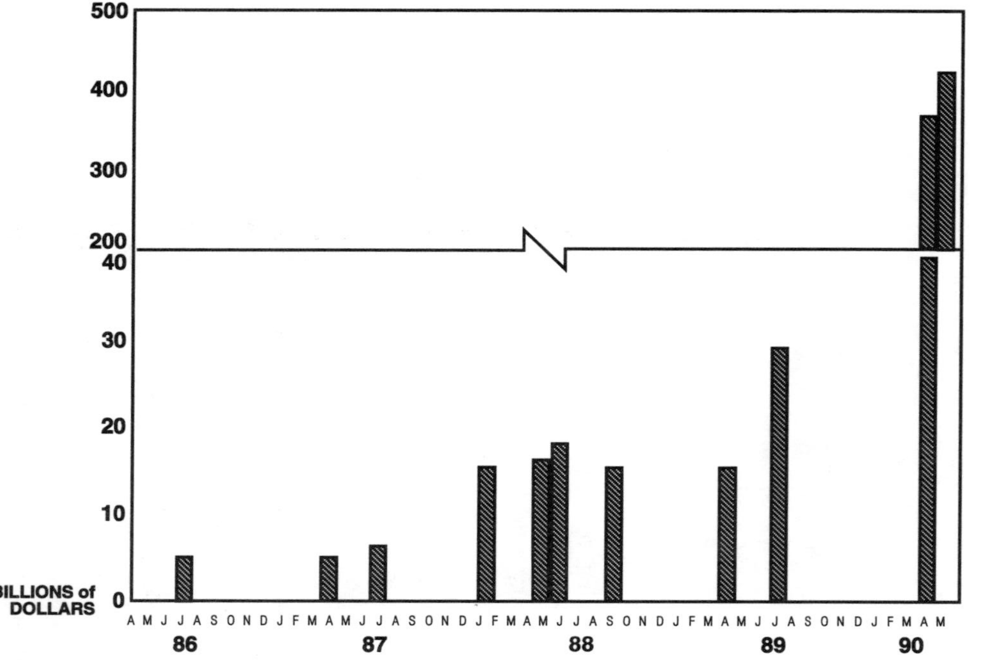

FIGURE A–1.—*Recovery cost estimate chronology through May 1990*

NOTES

Deterrence Before Chernobyl

1. The overwhelming majority of Japanese abhor even the thought of war. They still support their US-imposed constitutional limitation on offensive arms. Memories of their defeat in World War II, in particular the devastation created by two nuclear weapons, have shaped contemporary Japanese attitudes about military conflict. See: Robert C. Christopher, *The Japanese Mind* (New York: Linden Press, Simon and Schuster, 1983), 318; and William Sweet, *The Nuclear Age* (Washington, D.C.: Congressional Quarterly, Inc., 1988), 126. While the nuclear bombs at Hiroshima and Nagasaki did unprecedented damage, they did not scatter as much long-lived radioactive debris as Chernobyl. The atomic bombs were burst so high above ground that they didn't raise much dirt to mix with and carry the bombs' radioactive by-products. The Chernobyl reactor, on the other hand, contained a large quantity of long-lived radioactive particles that were lofted into the lower atmosphere almost continuously over the 10 days it took to snuff the reactor fire. Chapter 3 discusses more about the controversial comparison of Chernobyl's fallout to that of atmospheric nuclear weapon tests.

2. Michael Nacht, "Why Nuclear Deterrence Will Not Go Away." *Nuclear Deterrence,* ed. Catherine McArdle Kelleher, Frank J. Kerr, and George H. Quester (McLean, Va.: Pergammon-Brassey, 1986), 127.

3. Deterrence is hardly a new concept. Convincing the enemy not to even start a war is a psychological, even

a decisive, element of strategy discussed by Clausewitz. See: Andre Beaufre's analysis of deterrence and military strategy in *The Art and Practice of Military Strategy,* ed. George Edward Thibault (Washington, D.C.: National Defense University Press, 1984), 205. Louis C. Seelig defines US military and national strategies in *Resource Management in Peace and War* (Washington, D.C.: National Defense University Press, 1990), 43–44.

4. Steven Kull, *Minds At War* (New York: Basic Books, 1988), 279–280.

5. Different thought processes explain just one way deterrence could fail. Rational leaders could also miscalculate risks and benefits of agression. See: Keith B. Payne and Lawrence R. Fink, "Deterrence Without Defense: Gambling on Perfection," *Strategic Review* (Winter 1989): 26.

6. Tsuyoshi Hasegawa, "Soviets on Nuclear-War-Fighting," *Problems of Communism* XXXV (July-August 1986): 79.

7. Timothy J. Van Gelder, "Credible Threats and Usable Weapons: Some Dilemmas of Deterrence," *Philosophy and Public Affairs* 18, no. 2 (Spring 1989): 178, 179.

8. Roman Kolkowitz, "The Soviet Union: The Elusive Adversary," in *The Soviet Calculus of Nuclear War,* ed. Roman Kolkowitz and Ellen Propper Mickiewicz (Lexington, Mass.: Lexington Books, 1986), 7.

9. Colin S. Gray, *Nuclear Strategy and National Style* (Lanham, Md.: Hamilton Press, 1986), 88.

10. Dimitri K. Simes, "The Politics of Defense in the Soviet Union," *Soviet Decisionmaking for National Secu-*

rity, ed. Jiri Valenta and William C. Potter (London: George Allen and Unwin, 1984), 80.

11. Richard Pipes, "Why the Soviet Union Thinks It Could Fight and Win a Nuclear War," *Commentary* (July 1977): 29, 34. Pipes even goes so far as to say that the Soviets could "absorb the loss of 30 million of its people, and . . . emerge less hurt in terms of casualties than it was in 1945." (Pipes, 34). His opinion is significant because, unlike many US policy makers who crafted the national strategy of deterrence, he analyzed Soviet military writings in order to understand their attitudes about nuclear war. He makes it clear that the Soviet view is distinctly different from the US view. In contrast, Bernard Brodie's opinions have heavily influenced the US view of deterrence. He says that nuclear wars cannot be won, and that the chief purpose of the US military establishment must be to *avoid* wars. He calls Pipes' assessment of Soviet population survivability "an absurd notion." See: Bernard Brodie, "Development of Nuclear Strategy," *International Security* 2, no. 4 (Spring 1978): 65, 73.

12. Norman M. Naimark and David E. Powell, "Moscow's Cult of Militarism," *The National Interest,* no. 4 (Summer 1986): 53.

13. Leon Goure, *War Survival in Soviet Strategy* (Washington, D.C.: Center for Advanced International Studies, 1976), 2.

14. A. Gorokhov, "Battlefield Operations," *Pravda,* 20 May 1986, 1,6. Translation in *The Current Digest of the Soviet Press* XXXVIII, no. 24: 16. Incidentally, this revelation (25 days after the accident) of the Soviet military's involvement apparently contradicts a *New York City Tribune* allegation that the Soviet military's involve-

ment had been a secret until the *Tribune* revealed it 8 months later. See this book's epilogue, "After Chernobyl," for details of the military involvement, and note 8 for the *Tribune* references.

15. Kull, *Minds At War,* 276.

16. David Remnick, "Soviets Report 250 Deaths Occurred at Chernobyl," *Washington Post,* 9 November 1989, A70.

Chapter 1

1. Viktor Haynes and Marko Bojcun, *The Chernobyl Disaster* (London: The Hogarth Press, 1988). Haynes and Bojcun preface their self-proclaimed "indictment of nuclear power" with a biblical quotation (Revelations 8:10–11) identifying Wormwood as the star that falls from heaven into rivers and fountains of waters; many people died from the bitter waters. Wormwood is a plant whose name is synonymous with the bitterness of its oil.

2. Michael Dobbs, "Ukraine Stirs: Kremlin Shudders," *Washington Post,* 11 September 1989, A1, A18.

3. Maxim Rylsky, "The Nuclear Power Industry in the Ukraine," Interview with Vitali Sklyarov, Minister of Power and Electrification of the Ukraine, *Soviet Life* (February 1986): 8.

4. Maxim Rylsky, "A Town Born of the Atom," *Soviet Life* (February 1986): 7, 13. The *Soviet Life* article reflected a sense of confidence in their nuclear power industry that bordered on smugness. Marshall Goldman, Associate Director of the Harvard University Research Center, blames that smugness for their decision to design nuclear power plants without US-style containment vessels. Soviet designers have put containment vessels on

reactors that were built after the Three Mile Island accident. Chernobyl's reactors were obviously designed before that decision. See: Marshall I. Goldman, "Keeping the Cold war Out of Chernobyl," *Technology Review* (18 July 1986): 18.

5. Valeri Legasov, Lev Feokistov and Igor Kuzmin. "Nuclear Power Engineering and International Security," *Soviet Life* (February 1986): 14–15. In fact, there *were* other Soviet nuclear disasters; see Oberg (note 16) for a compilation. Legasov later stressed the need for better reactor safety programs after the Chernobyl accident (note 13).

6. B. I. Oleinik, "Appeal From Public for Review of Power Engineering Development in the Ukraine," speech printed in Pravda, 2 July 1988, 8. Translation in *The Current Digest of the Soviet Press* XL, no. 34: 12–13.

7. J.H. Gittus, and others, *The Chernobyl Accident and Its Consequences* (London: United Kingdom Atomic Energy Authority, March 1987). The RBMK acronym translation comes from the Soviet biologist/author Zhores Medvedev, in "The Road to Chernobyl," a chapter in *Politics After Chernobyl,* ed. Louis Mackay and Mark Thompson (London: Pluto Press, 1988), 17.

8. Richard Wilson, "A Visit To Chernobyl," *Science* 236 (June 26, 1987): 1636.

9. The description of the Soviet nuclear reactor is limited here to general information necessary to understand the scope of what happened at Chernobyl. Numerous technical accounts of the accident have been published, starting with the Soviets' own presentation at Vienna (*The Accident at the Chernobyl AES and Its Consequences,* 25–29 August 1986, Working Document for International Atomic Energy Agency Expert Conference,

US Department of Energy translation). The U.S. Nuclear Regulatory Commission's *Report on the Accident at the Chernobyl Nuclear Power Station,* NUREG–1250, Rev. 1, 1987, provides a very comprehensive technical description of the accident.

10. Victor G. Snell, "Introduction," in David R. Marples, *The Social Impact of the Chernobyl Accident* (New York: St. Martin's Press, 1988), 19.

11. A. Illesh, "Situation Under Control," *Izvestia,* 7 May 1986, 6. Translation in *The Current Digest of the Soviet Press* XXXVIII, no. 17: 4, 22–23.

12. The 31 casualties here refer to the number who died within a few weeks of the accident. Actually, hundreds were hospitalized with radiation sickness. As of late 1989, the death toll attributed to the Chernobyl accident was about 250. See: David Remnick, "Soviets Report 250 Deaths Occurred at Chernobyl," *Washington Post,* 9 November 1989, A70.

Twenty-six Chernobyl victims are buried outside Moscow at the Mitinskoye Cemetery. Six were firemen; the others were employees of the power station. They were to be honored with a monument; figure 1 shows its design, from F. Ivanov, "Monument to the Heroes of Chernobyl," *Izvestia,* 7 July 1988, 2. Translation in *The Current Digest of the Soviet Press* XL, no. 27: 23.

The monument relates the victims' suffering to nuclear technology using the symbol of an atmospheric nuclear weapon burst—a mushroom cloud. The monument has not yet been built, apparently because of fear that it could be misinterpreted as honoring the "bungling and negligence" that caused the accident in the first place. See: O. Dmitriyeva, "Do you Remember?" *Komsomolskaya Pravda,* 15 October 1987, 4. Translation in *The Current Digest of the Soviet Press* XXXIX, no. 43: 18.

The pictures of plant employees (referred to as "virtual criminals" in the Soviet press) were removed from gravestones at Mitinskoye Cemetery as a show of resentment toward those responsible for the disaster. The only operator's picture not removed from his grave was that of 26-year-old Leonid Toptunov. Figure 2 is a picture of his grave at Mitinskoye. He was young and inexperienced and not held personally accountable for the accident.

13. V. Legasov, "It Is My Duty To Tell About This," Pravda, 20 May 1988, 3, 8. Translation of extracts "From the Notes of Academician V. Legasov" in *National Affairs* published by the Foreign Broadcast Information Service, FBIS–SOV–88–098. Legasov was deputy director of the Kurchatov Institute for Nuclear Power, and member of the scientific team appointed by the Kremlin to investigate the Chernobyl accident. He headed the Soviet delegation to the Vienna conference (see note 9). Legasov, believed to be suffering from radiation sickness as a result of his work at Chernobyl, committed suicide in 1988.

14. V. Zhukovsky and V. Khrustov, "Water For Kiev," Sovetskaya Rossia, 9 July 1986, 4. Translation in *The Current Digest of the Soviet Press* XXXVIII, no. 34: 13–14.

15. "Chernobyl's Hard Lessons," *Pravda,* 1 August 1987, 6. Translation in *The Current Digest of the Soviet Press* XXXIX, no. 31: 23–24.

16. James E. Oberg, *Uncovering Soviet Disasters* (New York: Random House, 1988), 254.

17. Zh. Tkachenko, "As Duty Required," *Sotsialisticheskay Industria,* 11 May 1986, 4. Translation in *The Current Digest of the Soviet Press,* XXXVIII, no. 23: 14.

18. David Remnick, "Chernobyl's Coffin Bonus," *Washington Post,* 24 November 1989, A1, A50, A52.

19. *The Accident at Chernobyl and Its Consequences,* published by The State Committee for Using Atomic Energy in the USSR, and presented to the International Atomic Energy Agency Expert Conference, 25–29 August 1986, US Department of Energy translation, Appendix 7: 60.

20. S. Tsikora, "The Aftermath of Chernobyl," *Izvestia,* 10 February 1988, 2. Translation in *The Current Digest of the Soviet Press* XL, no. 6: 22.

21. L.R. Anspaugh, R.J. Catlin, and M. Goldman, "The Global Impact of the Chernobyl Reactor Accident," *Science* 242, no. 4885 (16 December 1988): 1517. "Collective dose commitment" is a way of expressing the aggregate of radiation doses received by a large number of people. It is used to correlate with the incidence of radiation effects, such as cancer, within the group.

22. R. Jeffrey Smith, "Low Level Radiation Causes More Deaths Than Assumed, Study Finds," *Washington Post,* 20 December 1989, A3.

23. Anspaugh, Catlin, and Goldman, *Global Impact,* 1518.

24. Pravda correspondent Vladimir Gubarev filed the first on-scene press reports from the Chernobyl accident site. His stage play, *Sarcophagus,* named after the popu-

lar name for the reactor's tomb, dramatizes many of the accident's events he witnessed and reported. The play openly criticizes authorities' indecisiveness in making evacuation decisions and creates a fictional version of the prosecution of the power station's former director. Scenes from the play were published in the 13 September 1986 issue of *Sovetskaya Kultura.* Translation is in *The Current Digest of the Soviet Press* XXXVIII, no. 38: 13–15.

25. Vladimir Zhukovsky, "What the Stir at the Kiev Bazaar is All About," Tass, 16 May 1986, 6. Translation in *The Current Digest of the Soviet Press* XXXVIII, no. 22: 16.

26. Dr. Robert Peter Gale and Thomas Houser, *Final Warning The Legacy of Chernobyl* (New York: Warner Books, 1988), 27. A Belorussian schoolteacher told Aleksandr Kondrasev, Belorussia's Deputy Minister of Public Health, about the "three Hiroshimas" comparison she learned at a lecture given to her machine operators club. S. Lyapich published their conversation in "According to Rumors, And Authoritatively: Radiation and Misinformation," *Sovetskaya Belorussia,* 9 August 1986, 3. Translation in *The Current Digest of the Soviet Press* XXXVIII, no. 36: 13. There is no precise, unambiguous way to compare the severity of the Chernobyl accident to the effects of a nuclear bomb of a specific yield. Published comparisons do vary tremendously. A bomb would undoubtedly kill a lot more people with its other effects, like airblast, heat, and prompt radiation. Fallout radiation comparisons generally examine the quantities of a few specific radionuclides that are created by the fission processes common to both. For example, see the next note, and: Richard Erskine and Philip Weber, "Accidents, Risks and Consequences," *Politics After*

Chernobyl, ed. Louis Mackay and Mark Thompson (London: Pluto Press, 1988), 46.

27. Cesium-137 is a radioactive element created by the fission process in bombs and reactors. Its radioactivity diminishes by half every 30 years (its half-life). Chernobyl liberated one tenth to one-sixth of the cesium-137 released by all atmospheric nuclear bombs, including Hiroshima and Nagasaki. See: Stuart Diamond, "Long-Term Chernobyl Fallout: Comparison to Bombs Altered," *New York Times,* 4 November 1986, C3.

28. US Nuclear Regulatory Commission, *Report on the Accident at the Chernobyl Power Station,* NUREG–1250, Rev. 1 (Washington, D.C.: US Government Printing Office, 1988), 6–2.

Chapter 2

1. Because the Soviets gave the world no warning, the radioactive plume's trajectory had to be computed retrospectively, using radiation detector data from a variety of Swedish locations and recorded wind data. Swedish scientists documented their analysis of radioactivity entering their country. See L. Devell and others, "Initial Observations of Fallout from the Reactor Accident at Chernobyl," *Nature* 321 (1986): 192–193.

2. Joyce Barnathan and others, "The Chernobyl Syndrome," *Newsweek,* 12 May 1986, 24. The Swedes traced the radioactive cloud's source to the Soviet Ukraine with help from scientists at the US Lawrence Livermore National Laboratory.

3. "From the USSR Council of Ministers," *Izvestia,* 30 April 1986, 1. Translation in *The Current Digest of the Soviet Press* XXXVIII, no. 16: 1.

4. Mr. Shcherbitsky was a Politburo member left over from the Brezhnev days. He was also accused of obstructing the process of *perestroika* in the Ukraine. See Associated Press, "Vladimir Shcherbitsky, 71, Ex-Politburo Member, Dies," *Washington Post,* 18 February 1990, D11. Four years after the accident, Ukrainian activists in Kiev demanded "criminal trials for those who failed to warn the populace about the radiation emanating from Chernobyl." See Reuter, "Ukrainians Mark Day of Chernobyl Disaster," *Washington Post,* 23 April 1990, A15.

5. Vera Rich, "Where Does the Blame Lie?," *Nature* 321 (15 May 1986): 187.

6. Viktor Haynes and Marko Bojcun, *The Chernobyl Disaster* (London: The Hogarth Press, 1988), 159.

7. V. Gubarev and M. Odinets, "The Station and Around It," *Pravda,* 6 May 1986, 6. Translation in *The Current Digest of the Soviet Press* XXXVIII, no. 17: 1–3.

8. Sallie Wise and Patricia Leroy, *The Chernobyl Disaster: Sources of Information and Reactions* (Washington, D.C.: Radio Free Europe/Radio Liberty, Audience and Opinion Research Report, AR 4–86, October 1986), 13.

9. Yury Zhukov, "Involuntary Self-Exposure," *Pravda,* 6 May 1986, 4. Translation in *The Current Digest of the Soviet Press* XXXVIII, no. 18: 5.

10. David R. Marples, *Chernobyl & Nuclear Power in the USSR* (New York, NY: St. Martin's Press, 1986), 8.

11. V. Gubarev and M. Odinets, "The Station and Around It," *Pravda,* 6 May 1986, 6. Translation in *The Current Digest of the Soviet Press* XXXVIII, no. 17: 62.

12. *East Europeans and the Chernobyl Events: Awareness, Primary Sources of Information and Attitudes Towards Soviet and Home Media Handling of Information* (Washington, D.C.: Radio Free Europe/Radio Liberty, East European Area Audience and Opinion Research Report Number 732, December 1986), 1.

13. Wise and Leroy, *The Chernobyl Disaster: Sources,* 6.

14. M.S. Gorbachev, Address on Soviet television printed in *Pravda* and *Izvestia,* 15 May 1986, 1. Translation in *The Current Digest of the Soviet Press* XXXVIII, no. 20: 19.

15. Ibid.

16. James E. Oberg, *Uncovering Soviet Disasters* (New York: Random House, 1988), 257.

17. Yury Zhukov, "Involuntary Self Exposure," *Pravda,* 6 May 1986, 4. Translation in *The Current Digest of the Soviet Press* XXXVIII, no. 18: 4.

18. Three Mile Island (TMI) was a ubiquitous topic in the Soviet media's damage limitation campaign. Gorbachev himself used it in his televised speech about Chernobyl on 15 May 1986. Actually, Chernobyl's environmental insult was much greater than TMI's. The US Nuclear Regulatory Commission estimated that approximately 100 *million* Curies of radionuclides were released from Chernobyl (see the *Report on the Accident at the Chernobyl Nuclear Power Station,* NUREG–1250–Rev–

1, 1988). A Curie is a measure of the rate at which a radioactive material emits photons of radiation or subatomic particles. One Curie is 37 billion such emissions per second. The Curie is named after the French scientists, Pierre and Madame Curie, whose pioneering efforts led to the isolation of the radioactive element radium.

About half of Chernobyl's release was in the form of chemically inert noble gases. Inert gases pose little direct threat to health because they don't react (and, therefore don't deposit themselves) readily in tissue. TMI's noble gas release was about one-fifth of Chernobyl's. On the other hand, Chernobyl released over a *million* times more radioactivity than TMI in the form of other, more dangerous elements. The relative insignificance of the TMI radioactivity release is consistent with the accident's cancer lethality forecast. One excess cancer death will probably result from TMI's contamination. Chernobyl's toll will probably number in the tens of thousands. See "Risks," in chapter 1, for more about Chernobyl's expected death toll. For technical discussions of the Chernobyl and TMI contamination, see: Colin Norman and David Dickson, "The Aftermath of Chernobyl," *Science,* 233 (12 September 1986): 1141, and Ronald Allen Knief, *Nuclear Energy Technology* (Washington, D.C.: Hemisphere Publishing Corporation, 1981), 441–443.

19. G. Arbatov, "Boomerang," *Pravda,* 9 May 1986, 4. Translation in *The Current Digest of the Soviet Press* XXXVIII, no. 19: 4.

20. "U.S. The Atlanta Suffers an Accident," *Izvestia,* 3 May 1986, 4. Translation in *The Current Digest of the Soviet Press* XXXVIII, no. 18: 1.

21. "Incident at Nuclear Proving Ground in Nevada," *Pravda,* 4 May 1986, 5. Translation in *The Current Digest of the Soviet Press* XXXVIII, no. 18: 2.

22. "Accidents at Atomic Power Stations," *Izvestia,* 5 May 1986, 4. Translation in *The Current Digest of the Soviet Press* XXXVIII, no. 18: 3.

23. V. Gan, "Auto Accident—Who Needed to Remove Karen Silkwood?," *Pravda,* 7 May 1986, 5. Translation in *The Current Digest of the Soviet Press* XXXVIII, no. 18: 9.

24. Vladimir Mikhailov, "Chernobyl and Hamm," *Pravda,* 4 June 1986, 5. Translation in *The Current Digest of the Soviet Press* XXXVIII, no. 31: 13.

25. "Accidents at Atomic Power Stations," *Izvestia,* 5 May 1986, 4. Translation in *The Current Digest of the Soviet Press* XXXVIII, no. 18: 4.

26. V. Gubarev and M. Odinets, "The Station and Around It," *Pravda,* 6 May 1986, 6. Translation in *The Current Digest of the Soviet Press* XXXVIII, no. 17: 2.

27. *Lenin Reader,* ed. Stephan T. Possony (Chicago: Henry Regnery Press, 1966), 101.

28. "On Events at the Chernobyl Power Station," *Pravda,* 7 May 1986, 3. Translation in *The Current Digest of the Soviet Press* XXXVIII, no. 18: 5.

29. Dr. Hans Blix, *The Post-Chernobyl Outlook for Nuclear Power* (Vienna, Austria: International Atomic Energy Agency Address to the European Nuclear Conference at Geneva, 1986), 9.

30. Leonard Tivey, "The Character of Nuclear Power Politics," *The Political Quarterly* 59, no. 4 (October-December 1988): 457.

31. David R. Marples, *The Social Impact of the Chernobyl Disaster* (New York: St. Martin's Press, 1988), xii.

32. Dr. Robert Peter Gale and Thomas Houser, *Final Warning The Legacy of Chernobyl* (New York: Warner Books, 1988), 204.

33. Christopher Flavin, *Reassessing Nuclear Power: The Fallout From Chernobyl* (Washington, D.C.: Worldwatch Institute Paper 75, March 1977), 58–59.

34. Bill Keller, "Soviet Scraps a New Atomic Plant in Face of Protest Over Chernobyl," *New York Times,* 28 January 1988, A1, A9.

35. Initially, the official Soviet response to Chernobyl was like their response to shooting down the Korean airliner, KAL007. "No information was provided until international pressure made the Soviets realize that silence was counterproductive." The difference was that Chernobyl occurred as their *glasnost* was transforming Soviet public relations policy away from isolationism. See: Ellen Jones and Benjamin L. Woodbury, "Chernobyl and Glasnost," *Problems of Communism* XXXV, no. 6 (November-December 1986): 28–38.

Chapter 3

1. Louis Mackay and Mark Thompson, "Introduction: Chernobyl and Beyond," in *Something in the Wind: Politics After Chernobyl,* ed. Louis Mackay and Mark Thompson (London: Pluto Press, 1988), 8.

2. Boris Oleinik, "The Main Guarantee," *Pravda,* 18 May 1986, 1. Translation in *The Current Digest of the Soviet Press* XXXVIII, no. 23: 16.

3. Mikhail Gorbachev, *Perestroika New Thinking For Our Country And The World* (New York: Harper and Row, 1988), 221–222. President Gorbachev describes his planned "revolution from above" to revitalize and purify the Soviet Union's quest to become a Leninist society. He uses Chernobyl as an example of how new thinking was applied to a real, contemporary problem, and resulted in an open, frank exchange with other countries. Of course, he doesn't mention his government's initial attempts to cover it up, then minimize the world's perception of the accident's scale. Chernobyl may have been too pervasive a disaster for any nation to hide. Ultimately, *glasnost* may have been the Soviets' only option.

4. Ibid., 221.

5. US Nuclear Regulatory Commission, *Implications of the Accident at Chernobyl for Safety Regulation of Commercial Nuclear Power Plants in the United States* (Washington, D.C.: US Nuclear Regulatory Commission, NUREG–1251, Volume 1, April 1989), 2. This document is the Commission's evaluation of how the Chernobyl accident should affect U.S. reactor regulation. It is based primarily on the Soviet data presented at the Vienna meetings in August, 1986, and the Commission's fact-finding report, NUREG 1250, Revision 1.

6. Colin Norman and David Dickson, "The Aftermath of Chernobyl," *Science* 233 (12 September 1986): 1141.

7. B. Sinelnikov, "Boomerang. Why There Are Few Good Documentary Films," *Pravda,* 16 July 1986, 6.

Translation in *The Current Digest of the Soviet Press* XXXVIII, no. 34: 14.

8. David R. Marples, *Chernobyl & Nuclear Power in the USSR* (New York, NY: St. Martin's Press, 1986), 12.

9. *Tygodnik Muzowsze,* 15 May 1986, quoted by Mark Thompson, "Lines of Latitude: People's Detente, East and West," in *Something in the Wind: Politics After Chernobyl,* ed. Louis Mackay and Mark Thompson (London: Pluto Press, 1988), 108.

10. Grigoriy Medvedev, "Incompetence; Pages From the Chernobyl Notebook," *Kommunist,* no. 4 (March 1989): 93–105. Translation in Joint Publications Research Service document JPRS–UKO–89–010, 9 June 1989: 69.

11. Ibid., 75.

12. Ibid., 76.

13. Valerii Legasov, "The Pain and Lessons of Chernobyl," interview by V. Gubarev, *Pravda,* 2 June 1986, 7. Translation in *The Current Digest of the Soviet Press* XXXVIII, no. 28: 12.

14. Valerii Legasov, "A Soviet Expert Discusses Chernobyl," interview by Nikolai Vikh'yayev (Novosti Press Agency, April 1987), published in *Bulletin of the Atomic Scientists* (July/August 1987): 32.

15. Valerii Legasov, "It Is My Duty to Tell About This," *Pravda,* 20 May 1988, 3. Translation in *The Current Digest of the Soviet Press* XL, no. 20: 13.

16. Vera Rich, "Legasov's Indictment of Chernobyl Management," *Nature* 333 (26 May 1988): 285.

17. Aleksandr Levada, "The Pripyat is My Moorage," *The Soviet Review* XXVII, no. 2 (Summer 1987): 6.

18. A. Protsenko, "Nuclear Power After Chernobyl," *Pravda,* 6 September 1988, 3. Translation in *National Affairs* FBIS–SOV–88–177 (13 September 1988): 57.

19. R. Jeffrey Smith, "Soviets to Close Major Site of Underground Atomic Tests," *The Washington Post,* 17 March 1990, A1, A19.

20. Steven Kull, *Minds At War* (New York, NY: Basic Books Inc., 1988), 37. Kull's work explores the psychological aspects of US and Soviet defense policy formulation. Through a series of interviews with key officials, Kull derives support for his hypothesis that the "nuclear reality" has caused inconsistencies in the way policymakers think about deterrence and nuclear war. For example, he asks how military planners can justify the development of nuclear "war winning" plans while they admit that winning would be a grotesque distortion of the concept of victory. Stanford University's Center for International Security and Arms Control supported Kull's interesting and unusual psychoanalyses of deterrent thought processes.

Chapter 4

1. Leon Goure, *War Survival in Soviet Strategy* (Washington, D.C.: Center For Advanced International Study, 1976), 6–7. Dr. Goure is the Director of the Center for Soviet Studies at Science Applications International Corporation in McLean, Virginia. In addition to his assessments of Soviet civil defense, Dr. Goure has extensively analyzed Soviet military strategy and performance, including their response to Chernobyl.

2. An articulate summary of the "fight and win" position is Harvard University professor Richard Pipes' "Why the Soviet Union Thinks It Could Fight and Win a Nuclear War," *Commentary,* July 1977.

3. Ibid., 10.

4. Federal Emergency Management Agency (FEMA), *Soviet Civil Defense* (Washington, D.C.: FEMA–52, December 1983), 2–3. Based on "research conducted by the U.S. Intelligence Community" this document is FEMA's estimate of the extent and potential effectiveness of the Soviet civil defense program.

5. Ibid., 18.

6. The stress of Chernobyl can only be considered "benign" in direct comparison to the stress that might be imposed by a nuclear war. The hypothetical contamination from thousands of nuclear bomb bursts would surely dwarf the tragic effects of a nuclear reactor accident. This is not to minimize perceptions of the severity of the Chernobyl accident. Rather, it is to help comprehend the task of a civil defense system that is responsible for societal survival and recovery from nuclear war.

7. William C. Potter, *Soviet Decisionmaking for Chernobyl: An Analysis of System Performance and Policy Change* (Washington, D.C.: The National Council for Soviet and East European Research, March 1990), ii, 60.

8. Lt. Gen. N. Bondarchuk, "Strict Accounting," Interview with Chief of Staff of the Ukrainian Civil Defense, by V. Mironov, *Voyennyye Znaniya,* no. 12 (December 1987): 10–11. Translation in Joint Publications Research Service JPRS—UMA–88–006 (28 March 1988): 57–59.

9. Ibid., 58.

10. Col. Gen. A. Ryakhov, "Civil Defense" The Restructuring Depends Upon Each of Us," *Voyennyye Znaniya,* no. 12 (December 1987): 8–9. Translation in Joint Publications Research Service JPRS–UMA–88–006 (28 March 1988): 62.

11. V. Ptitsyna, "The Games Adults Play," *Twentieth Century And Peace,* No. 10, 1987, pp. 7, 47. Translation in Joint Publications Research Service JPRS–UMA–88–003 (23 February 1988): 32.

12. Lt. Gen. M. Maksimov, "For Those Who Perform the Training: One of Chemistry's 'Jobs'," *Voyennyye Znaniya,* no. 11 (November 1987) 28–29. Translation in Joint Publications Research Service JPRS–UMA–88–006 (28 March 1988): 64.

13. S. Tsikora, "The Aftermath of Chernobyl," *Izvestia,* 10 February 1988, 2. Translation in *The Current Digest of the Soviet Press* XL, no. 6: 22–23.

14. The Soviet press contains numerous articles that expose and try to debunk popular beliefs in the benefits of alcohol mixtures for radiation protection. The Soviet Union's widespread alcoholism problems probably made such folk remedies believable and attractive to many people. According to the Vice Chairman of Moscow's City Soviet Executive Committee, the average male Muscovite stands in line for about 80 hours a year to buy alcohol. Maintaining order in those lines requires the efforts of 400 police and volunteer aides each day. See: V. Belikov, "End of Wine Line is in Sight," *Izvestia,* 3 October 1988, 1. Translation in *The Current Digest of the Soviet Press* XL, no. 40: 29. A. Pokrovsky wrote about the vodka and iodine anti-radiation potion in

"Zone of Increased Attention," *Pravda,* 5 June 1986, 3. Translation in *The Current Digest of the Soviet Press* XXXVIII, no. 31: 13–14. The vodka and red wine story came from O.P. Shchepin, the USSR's First Deputy Minister of Public Health, in an interview by G. Podgurskaya and V. Sharov, "Learning From Misfortune," *Literatunaya Gazeta,* 21 May 1986, 10. Translation in *The Current Digest of the Soviet Press* XXXVIII, no. 25: 14. V. Itkin and other Tass correspondents reported the rumor about Kiev's cut-rate liquor sales (as well as the "cock and bull" quote from Ivashchenko) in their article "Patrol in the Danger Zone," *Sovetskaya Rossia,* 10 June 1986, 4. Translation in *The Current Digest of the Soviet Press* XXXVIII, no. 32: 12.

15. The Soviets are preparing to formally release detailed technical information about the Kyshtym chemical explosion and the extent of the radioactive contamination that it produced. The International Atomic Energy Agency will receive the report as they work with the Soviets to orchestrate international support for the Chernobyl cleanup and aftereffects' studies. In another stunning example of *glasnost,* a Soviet militia Colonel described the cover-up of a nuclear power plant accident that happened at Beloyarskaya 8 years before Chernobyl. He said that it was a "moral crime to keep the accident a secret." See: V. Kaminchik, "Paper Reports Nuclear Accident After 10 Years," *Socialisticheskaya Industriya,* 21 October 1988. Translation in *National Affairs* FBIS–SOV–88–206 (25 October 1988): 58. More examples of Soviet coverup attempts are in James E. Oberg's book: *Uncovering Soviet Disasters* (New York: Random House, 1988), 257.

16. Angelina Konstantinovna Guskova (a hospital official where gravely ill patients were cared for) interviewed

by Alimov and A. Illesh. "The Pain of Chernobyl," *Izvestia,* 28 May 1986, 6. Translation in *The Current Digest of the Soviet Press* XXXVIII, no. 27: 17.

17. Ibid., 17.

18. K.I. Gordeyev, *Sovetskaya Belorussia,* 14 April 1987, 3. Translation in *The Current Digest of the Soviet Press* XXXIX, no. 17: 4. Soviet public health officials originally claimed that the fallout radiation levels at Khoiniki were not hazardous. They said that children had been evacuated "for recreation." See: N. Ye. Savchenko interviewed by A. Pryanishnikov, "At Your Request: Once More About Radiation and Safety," *Sovetskaya Belorussia,* 8 June 1986, 4. Translation in *The Current Digest of the Soviet Press* XXXVIII, no. 32: 11. In 1989, Ales Adamovich, a writer and Soviet People's Deputy, declared that Khoiniki had received dangerous levels of radioactive contamination from Chernobyl, and that "no agriculture should be conducted there." See: "Crimes in the Time of Restructuring: The Big Lie,: *Moskovskiye Novosti,* Round Table Discussion, 15 October 1989, 8–9. Translation in *The Current Digest of the Soviet Press* XLI, no. 44: 4.

19. As mentioned in Chapter 1, many experts now believe that there could ultimately be *tens* of thousands of cancer fatalities caused by Chernobyl's widespread radioactive contamination. It is a technicality on the Soviets' part to disagree with the experts' lethality projection on the question of whether the deaths will all occur by the year 2000. See Jeffrey R. Smith, "Low Level Radiation Causes More Deaths Than Assumed, Study Finds," *Washington Post,* 20 December 1989, A3. The National Research Council's *Health Effects of Exposure to Low Levels of Ionizing Radiation, BEIR V,* refutes the Soviets' argument about low radiation doses: it says that no radi-

ation dose is risk free. *BEIR V* was published by the National Academy Press, Washington, D.C., in 1990. Incidentally, the US National Research Council's findings are also seemingly at odds with the US Nuclear Regulatory Commission (NRC). The NRC's policy of "below regulatory concern" would deregulate some very low level radioactive wastes, permitting them to be handled, disposed, or even recycled into consumer products like nonradioactive materials are.

20. Lt. Gen. M. Maksimov, "For Those Who Perform the Training: One of Chemistry's 'Jobs'," 64–65.

21. V. Senchikhin, "Methods of Maintaining Livestock in Zones of Radioactive Contamination," *Voyennyye Znaniya,* March 1989, 42–43. Translation in Joint Publications Research Service JPRS–UMA–89–012 (22 May 1989): 58–60.

22. V. Shevtsov, "Complex Objective," *Voyennyye Znaniya,* January 1987, 14–15. Translation in Joint Publications Research Service JPRS–UMA–87–027 (May 1987): 60.

23. Ibid., 61.

24. S. Blagovolin, "The Strength and Impotence of Military Might: Is an Armed Conflict Between East and West a Real Possibility in Our Time?," *Izvestia,* 18 November 1988, 5. Translation in *The Current Digest of the Soviet Press* XL, no. 46: 3.

25. Soviet President Gorbachev talked about reactor attacks in an after-dinner speech to French President Mitterrand, at the Kremlin on July 7, 1986, barely three months after Chernobyl's fires had been extinguished. *Pravda* published Gorbachev's text in an article entitled

"In a Friendly Atmosphere," 8 July 1986, 2. Translation in *The Current Digest of the Soviet Press* XXXVIII, no. 27: 5.

26. Albert L. Weeks, "Soviet Military's Post-Chernobyl Role Revealed as Officers Receive Honors," *New York City Tribune,* 27 January 1987, 1. Mr. Weeks cites "well known defense analyst Dr. Joseph D. Douglas" (City Tribune, also) when he asserts that the Soviets already have reserve, underground nuclear power reactors ready to provide electricity if the aboveground plants are destroyed. Bennett Ramberg actually reasons that deterrence would be *enhanced* if the West adopted a policy of targeting Soviet nuclear reactors. See: *Nuclear Power Plants as Weapons for the Enemy* (Berkeley: University of California Press, 1980), xxvi, 74.

27. Dr. Sally Leivesley, "Chernobyl: The Invisible Threat," *RUSI (Royal United Services Institute For Defence Studies) Journal* (Summer 1988): 41.

Chapter 5

1. "Detailed Study of Chernobyl Set," *International Herald Tribune,* 12–13 May 1990, 5. The International Atomic Energy Agency is planning to send 100 specialists to the Soviet Union to evaluate the long-term aspects of the accident, and to help the Soviets improve disaster response planning. Such assistance is in the world's best interest, because, in the words of Dr. Robert Gale (*60 Minutes,* transcript XXII, no. 22 [18 February 1990]: 4) the Soviet Union is "a technologically unsophisticated society playing with fire." In another profound example of international involvement and cooperation, the Soviets are letting a group of world experts actually decide the fate of a Gorkii nuclear station. See: "Experts to Decide Fate of Nuclear Station," Tass, 29 August 1989. Trans-

lation in Joint Publications Research Service JPRS–TND–89–018 (18 September 1989): 34.

2. "Diplomatic Conference on Reaffirmation and Development of International Humanitarian Law Applicable in Armed Conflict: Protocols I and II to the Geneva Conventions," Reproduced from United Nations Document A/32/144 dated 15 August 1977, and published in *International Legal Materials* 16 (1977): 1391–1449. Article 56, "Protection of Works and Installations Containing Dangerous Forces," is on page 1415.

3. "Soviets Ratify 1977 Protocols to Geneva Pact," *New York Times,* 17 August 1989, I–15. The Supreme Soviet unanimously ratified the Protocols at the Kremlin on 4 August 1989.

4. Richard Masters, "Chernobyl Has Less-Than-Expected Impact on Orders and Future Plans," *Nuclear Engineering International* 32 (June 1987): 28.

5. Guy B. Roberts, "The New Rules For Waging War: The Case Against Ratification of Additional Protocol I," *Virginia Journal of International Law* 20, no. 1 (Fall 1985): 118.

6. Ibid., 157.

7. "Soviets Ratify 1977 Protocols to Geneva Pact," *New York Times,* 17 August 1989, I–15.

8. Valerii Legasov, interviewed by Ales Adamovich, " 'I Give My Word, No More Explosions,' or The Opinion of a Non-Specialist," *Novy Mir,* no. 9 (September 1988): 164–179. Translation in *The Current Digest of the Soviet Press* XL, no. 42: 1.

9. V. Ptitsyna, "The Games Adults Play," *Twentieth Century and Peace,* no. 10: 7, 47. Translation in Joint Publications Research Service JPRS–UMA–88–003 (23 February 1988): 32.

10. *The Accident at the Chernobyl AES and Its Medical Consequences,* 25–29 August 1986, Working Document for the International Atomic Energy Agency Expert Conference, US Department of Energy translation: Appendix 7, "Medical and Biological Problems," Part I, p. 44.

11. "U.S. Care For Chernobyl Hero," *New York Times,* 14 April 1990, 7. "Anatoly Grishchenko, Chernobyl Victim, 43," *New York Times,* 4 July 1990, 13.

12. "Chernobyl Hunger Strike," *Washington Post,* 31 March 1990, A21.

13. Dr. Hans Blix, interviewed by V. Gubarev and B. Dubrovin, "In the Mirror of Chernobyl—An Interview With Dr. Hans Blix," *Pravda,* 24 April 1987, 6. Translation in *The Current Digest of the Soviet Press* XXXIX, no. 17: 4. Dr. Blix heads the International Atomic Energy Agency (IAEA). The IAEA is a nuclear industry advocates' club. Its Deputy Director is a Soviet government official. It is interesting that Dr. Blix praises Soviet *glasnost* a year after the accident, while the Soviet report to Vienna (August 1986) was not released to the Soviets' own scientific community. See: Viktor Haynes and Marko Bojcun, *The Chernobyl Disaster* (London: The Hogarth Press, 1988), 197.

14. A. Ivakhov, "Atomic Power Stations Today and Tomorrow," *Izvestia,* 9 December 1987, 3. Translation in *The Current Digest of the Soviet Press* XXXIX, no. 49: 9.

15. G. Arbatov, "Boomerang," *Pravda,* 9 May 1986, 4. Translation in *The Current Digest of the Soviet Press* XXXVIII, no. 19: 4.

16. Ye. P. Velikhov, "Chernobyl Warns," *Pravda,* 27 May 1986, 5. Translation in *The Current Digest of the Soviet Press* XXXVIII, no. 27: 15.

17. Vladimir Sokolov, interviewed by Kim Smirnov, "Where Should Robinson Crusoe Settle?," *Izvestia,* 4 June 1986, 3. Translation in *The Current Digest of the Soviet Press* XXXVIII, no. 31: 13.

18. Yury Shcherbak, "Without Conjectures or Innuendos," *Literatunaya Gazeta,* 23 July 1986, 11. Translation in *The Current Digest of the Soviet Press* XXXVIII, no. 35: 12.

19. Vasily Chigryai, interviewed by Elizabeth Shogren, "Four Years Later, Chernobyl's Ills Widen," *Washington Post,* 27 April 1990, 1.

Chapter 6

1. Viktor Haynes and Marko Bojcun, *The Chernobyl Disaster* (London: The Hogarth Press, 1988), 49.

2. Sally Leivesley, "Chernobyl: The Invisible Threat," *RUSI (Royal United Services Institute For Defense Studies) Journal* (Summer 1988): 41.

3. "Byelorussians Say Evacuation From Chernobyl Zones is Urgent," *Nucleonics Week* (22 March 1990): 6.

4. Yu. Shcherbak, a Kiev writer, ecologist, and nuclear safety investigator, quoted by Yevgina Albats at a "Post-Chernobyl Round Table Discussion of Crimes During

Perestroika," *Moskovskiye Novosti,* 15 October 1989, 8–9. Translation in *The Current Digest of the Soviet Press* XLI, no. 44: 1.

5. Ibid., 4. Quote is from Ales Adamovich at the same "Round Table Discussion."

6. Stanislav Kondrashov, "Once More About the Caribbean Crisis," *Izvestia,* 28 February 1989, 5. Translation in *The Current Digest of the Soviet Press* XLI, no. 9: 1–4.

7. Paul Marantz, "Soviet 'New Thinking' and East-West Relations," *Current History* (October 1988): 311–312.

8. Albert L. Weeks, "Soviet Military's Post-Chernobyl Role Revealed as Officers Receive Honors," *New York City Tribune* (27 January 1987): 1. Weeks claims that Soviet military involvement at Chernobyl was a secret for the first 8 months after the accident, and that the extent of their participation was partially revealed when the military newspaper, Red Star, announced that the head of the Chemical Defense troops, Colonel-General Pikalov, had been awarded the Soviet Union's highest award, the Order of Lenin, for his performance at Chernobyl. Weeks apparently didn't see the 20 May 1986 Pravda story about how Soviet Chemical and Civil Defense military troops had assumed a substantial role in the cleanup job. See: A. Gorokov, "Battlefield Operations," *Pravda,* 20 May 1986, 1,6. Translation in *The Current Digest of the Soviet Press* XXXVIII, no. 24: 16. Pikalov narrated his own account in an interview with Lieutenant-Colonel Valentin Perov, "Chernobyl One Year Later," *Soviet Military Review,* no. 5 (May 1987): 45–46. The fact that Red Army Reserves were used in the cleanup was mentioned to the author by a Red Army officer at a meeting between National Defense University

students and Soviet military officers in Volgograd, USSR, on 8 May 1990.

9. Perov, 46.

10. Ibid.

Index

The Author

Lieutenant Colonel Arthur T. Hopkins, US Air Force, wrote this book while he was a Research Fellow at the National Defense University and a student at the Industrial College of the Armed Forces. Before studying at the National Defense University, he was assigned to the Air Force Center for Studies and Analyses in the Pentagon, where he analyzed strategic missile performance and the effects of nuclear weapons. His Air Force career includes project management positions at the Aeronautical Systems Division, Headquarters, Defense Nuclear Agency, and the Space and Missile Systems Organization.

LtCol Hopkins earned his Ph.D. and Master's Degree in Nuclear Engineering at the Air Force Institute of Technology. In addition, he holds Bachelor and Master of Science degrees in Aerospace and Atmospheric Sciences from the Catholic University of America. LtCol Hopkins has written and published numerous technical journal articles and study reports on a variety of topics, including reentry aerodynamics, mobile missile operations, and the numerical simulation of nuclear fallout transport. He is a member of the American Nuclear Society, the Health Physics Society, and the Military Operations Research Society.

LtCol Hopkins is currently Staff Scientist and Chief of the Scientific and Technical Analysis Branch of the Concepts Division in the Joint Strategic Target Planning Staff, Offutt Air Force Base, NE.

☆ U.S. G.P.O:1994-301-304/00001